Just Call Me Darcelle
A Memoir

Walter Cole
with Sharon Knorr

©2010 All rights reserved

This book is dedicated to Roxy and my loving family.
Without their love, the pages of this book would be blank.

Acknowledgements
Co-Author – Sharon Knorr
Book Inspiration – Barbara Dunn
Cover/Back Cover Photos/photos – Marvin Pierson
Publicist/Graphic Art/photos – Kimberlee Van Patten
Photos – Jan Haaken
Photos – Maridee Woodson
Editor – Jill Kelly
Book Design/Layout – Amy Livingstone

Just Call Me Darcelle was first a one-man show written by me and Sharon Knorr and directed by Sharon. I thank everyone at the club, the video crew who worked on the DVD, and all the audiences that came to the show for helping us make that a successful project. It is from that show that this book was born.

TABLE OF CONTENTS

Prologue	1
Chapter 1. *One foot in front of the other*	5
Chapter 2. *Linnton, when it was a town*	15
Chapter 3. *Lipstick, lashes, and Barbra*	25
Chapter 4. *My guardian angel*	33
Chapter 5. *Don't tell, don't tell anyone*	39
Chapter 6. *Luck and urban renewal*	69
Chapter 7. *There comes a time*	93
Chapter 8. *My life with Roxy*	103
Chapter 9. *World tours*	111
Chapter 10. *What's in a name?*	121
Epilogue	131

PROLOGUE
Countdown to Carnegie Hall Concert

"Wow, what a hell of a night for a shy little boy from Linnton, Oregon to be on stage with Thomas Lauderdale, Storm Large, Carlos Kalmar, and the Oregon Symphony with this wonderful audience... all because I wear a dress."

—*Darcelle*

At the end of July, the most gifted pianist in the world, Thomas Lauderdale of Pink Martini fame, called and asked if I would like to sing with the Oregon Symphony. After a half-a-second pause, I said, "Yes! Yes! Yes!"

I don't sing. Well I do sing one song, "The Rose," but I have had years and years of practice.

Thomas told me to come to his studio and we would find a key for me to do the song in. Oh sure, easy for him to say.

So a couple of days later, Roxy and I drove to Second Avenue and parked the car. To say I was nervous is an understatement. Into the studio we went.

Thomas played and I sang. We found a key… well, he found a key. The song was "New York, New York." I felt like I was hardly "singing" it but Thomas was a doll and made me feel at ease. We worked for about an hour and made dates for more rehearsal time together.

When it was time to leave, I couldn't find my car keys. We tore his place apart. Nothing. Thomas gladly ran outside to see if I had left them in the car. He came back in and announced that the car was running with the keys in it. It had been running the whole hour long. Oh brother, sure I was fine. In any other city than Portland, we would have not had a car.

Storm Large was to sing several songs on the symphony night and then we were going to end the show singing "New York, New York" together. So she came to a couple of our next rehearsals with her great voice and she too made me feel very at ease.

The concert was on September 18, 2010, and the day before that we had a rehearsal with Carlos and the entire orchestra…all 75 members. I walked into the hall, stood at the bottom of the stage, and announced to the group: "I'm scared!"

Everyone on stage started talking. "Don't be afraid. You'll be fine."

Okay, September 18. Arlene Schnitzer Concert Hall. This was it. By that time, I had no nerves, just a feeling of awe that Darcelle had been asked to do this and it had come together. I was probably floating a foot above the ground. All I could think about was all the shows I had been in…local theater book plays, hundreds of shows at the DarcelleXV showplace, shows all over the country, and personal appearances and fundraisers for many, many important causes and important people. But at this moment, I was indeed "king of the hill, top of the list, cream of the crop… number 1."

The show was coming to the end. I was waiting in the wings while Storm finished her songs to a standing ovation. My family and friends were in the audience. Thomas had told me just before his entrance to say something when I got on stage. Storm said some nice things about me and introduced me. I stepped out on stage and the place went nuts. Everyone was on their feet applauding and shouting words of love. It was all I could do to get the next part out.

"Wow, what a hell of a night for a shy little boy from Linnton, Oregon to be on stage with Thomas Lauderdale, Storm Large, Carlos Kalmar, and the Oregon Symphony and this wonderful audience… all because I wear a dress."

Then Thomas started playing the opening: "Start spreading the news…" Storm took a step back and said, "Take it!"

I sang the first two verses alone…on top of the world. Every note, every word perfect. Angels wings were certainly holding me up. Storm joined in and we did a show-stopping finish.

Then another standing ovation, applause, tears and love came across the footlights. As if that was not enough, Storm mentioned that my big birthday was coming up and so everyone in the room sang "Happy Birthday" with Thomas Lauderdale's accompaniment. It was the highlight of my career and a peak moment in my life.

My daughter Maridee came up to the edge of the stage and called up to me, "I have never seen you so happy on stage."

CHAPTER 1
One foot in front of the other

The first time I put on a dress, I was 37. My friend Roxy invited me to a Halloween costume ball at the Hoyt Hotel where he worked.

He said to me, "You will dress up and I will paint you." (That's drag talk for doing my makeup.)

"Uuuuhhhh…Okay," I said.

On the afternoon of the party, I showed up at his apartment. On the dining room table, there was a towel spread out and on the towel were little bottles, small containers, tubes, compacts, sponges, brushes of all shapes and sizes, and a bowl of water. It looked like an alchemist's ingredients for the universal elixir or the preparations for major surgery.

He told me to sit down.

"Uuuuhhhh…Okay."

First he took a sponge, wet it in the water, dunked it in a pot of skin-colored gunk, and came toward my face.

"Ok, first we put on base. This is the canvas that all the other make-up will go on. It is water-soluble… we put it on with water and it will wash off with water so don't worry about that part."

I had done some theater, so I knew what base was, but this was different from the grease paint I had used before. The sponge hit my face like an ice cube.

"Ouch… it's cold. Can't you use warm water"

Roxy started rubbing the sponge all over my face a little harder than I thought necessary. "Sit still and quit being such a baby," he said.

"Fine, but do you have to be so rough?"

"I'm trying to cover the wrinkles."

"WRINKLES!"

Next he picked up a pot of the bluest blue powder I had ever seen, grabbed a small brush, and again came at me.

"Now eye shadow…"

"Wow…that is really BLUE…" I said, and like a smart ass, I asked, "What do you call that shade? Periwinkle?"

"Very funny. Sit still and close your eyes."

The brush tickled.

"Ahh, careful!"

"Quit twitching. Hold still…there…very good. Okay. Next is eyeliner…keep your eyes closed…eyes closed!"

He had a very small brush and was painting black at the edge of my eyelashes, upper and lower and that really made me squirm.

"OK, now look up…down…up…down…DOWN!"

"God stop! I'm getting dizzy and it itches."

"DON'T TOUCH YOUR EYES!"

"Okay, okay."

"Next, eyelashes."

"I have eyelashes."

"Not like these."

And out of a little box he produced lashes that would have made Liza Minnelli back away.

"Close your eyes…close your eyes…KEEP THEM CLOSED…the glue has to dry. Wait, wait, wait! Okay, open your eyes."

Slowly I opened both eyes. "Hey! This one is glued shut!"

"DON'T TOUCH YOUR EYES. I'll get it…I'll get it. Okay, there…now you have eyelashes."

"Yeah, well I don't have any on the bottom of this eye anymore."

"Shut up… Now lipstick!"

On the table were pots and tubes and sticks of every color of red imaginable. How in the world did women do this every day? Too many choices. And he was going to use a brush not just a lipstick tube.

"Open your mouth…keep it open…OPEN! Okay."

He tipped the brush into a pot and started painting it on like spackle.

"Now shmush your lips back and forth."

That I could do. I had seen enough women doing it…but nevertheless it felt very strange.

"Good. Now take your fingers and wipe off the excess by the edges of your mouth…yes…there. Great! Perfect!"

Then he took a medium-sized brush and spread color from another pot all over my cheeks. He took a dark pencil and colored in my eyebrows in places where I don't think I naturally had eyebrows. He took a huge brush and covered my face in sheer powder to "set it," he said. I thought I was in a dust storm and kept snorting so it would stop going up my nose.

He took a step back, looked me up and down with a pleased smile, then handed me a mirror and announced, "Voilà! YOU LOOK FABULOUS!"

I blinked in the mirror and he was right. I did look fabulous.

"Wow, what time is it?" I asked.

"5:30."

"Gee, that only took 2 hours." Another smart-ass remark.

Next it was time for the costume. Roxy had borrowed it from the costume shop at the Hoyt Hotel and it was in a pile on the couch. First he handed me a package that held black fishnet stockings. I took them out of the plastic and held them up. They looked like they would fit a midget.

"What the hell am I supposed to do with these?"

"Put them on," he shot back at me with a disgusted look.

"HOW?"

"Oh for heaven sakes…here…you roll up each side one at a time in your hands, then you stick your foot in and pull them up your leg."

"Are you kidding? I'm six feet tall."

But I did what he said and after a lot of struggle they made it all the way to my waist even though I felt like they could spring right back down at any moment. I will admit, however, they looked very sexy on, very sexy. Although later, when I took them off, I had waffle butt. It looked like I had a disease.

Then came a leotard…in this case a French-cut leotard. Now a French cut is like a tank top with a butt floss on it. It is cut very high on the sides and there is nothing covering your butt. The front is very small and fits tight. They are made for women, not large men. I was so tucked and pulled into that thing that my tits weren't my tits, they were my balls. Whew! I was going to be worn out before we even left.

Next Roxy handed me what looked like a very big, very long apron with ruffles all over it.

"What is THIS?"

"It's a skirt that you tie around your waist in the front so that the ruffles cascade down the back like a train."

Well at least it covered my bare waffle-squared butt!

As the last piece, I put on a very tall black wig with red flowers up one side. And there I was: a tall statuesque Flamenco dancer with very red lips. And I looked wonderful—at least to me I did.

Okay, now for the shoes. As a man, I wear size 10 in men's shoes. Where in the world do you find women's shoes, especially high-heeled women's shoes, that will fit?

One answer…Goodwill. Size 12 petite Springolators.

"Now walk," Roxy ordered me.

"Uuuuhhhh…okay."

All of us, men and women alike, tried on our mother's high heels and walked around the house. I'm sure there is a photo in every family scrapbook of the toddler in high heels, usually a naked toddler in high heels that we like to show to our teenager's prom date. But when you are a grown-up man and you walk in high heels for the first time, you tend to walk like a linebacker.

Roxy became a drill sergeant as I wobbled up and down the hall and around the table reaching out for support. "Keep your ankles together. You could drive a MAC truck through your legs. Stand up straight… don't hold on to the furniture. On your toes…ON YOUR TOES! Don't put weight on the heels until you learn how to do this. Tippy toe…TIPPY TOE!"

On I went, one foot in front of the other. One foot in front of the other.

An hour and a half later, we were ready to go to the ball—in Roxy's Karman Ghia. I climbed into the car headfirst. "I'm facing the wrong way."

I got turned around and Roxy yelled, "Don't sit on the ruffles!"

Oh for God's sake. So I held the wig on my lap, threw the ruffled train over my head, and away we went.

"Roxy, you'll have to tell me when we get there…All I can see is black hair and rosebuds."

When we arrived in front of the hotel, I asked Roxy to make sure there was no one looking as I unfolded myself out of the car onto the sidewalk so I could put on my wig. As I stood up…there were 40 people in line to get in the door. Never fails.

Now the Hoyt Hotel was quite the place. Harvey Dick, a prominent Portland man, had bought an old skid-row hotel and transformed it into a wonderland.

There was a men's bar done in precise period décor of the 1890's. Real gas lights on the walls and no stools at the bar, just a brass rung around the bottom where a man could stand, maybe to put one boot up on it if he wanted. I think that is where the expression "Belly up to the bar, boys" came from. Under their feet was a grate in the floor where a stream of water ran all the time so that after much drink, patrons could just un-button and relieve themselves right there. They never had to give up their place at the bar. In my day, the image remained.

The main room of the hotel was a huge ballroom called the Roaring 20s Room. It had rococo gilded ceilings and mirrors covering all the walls, amazing chandeliers, and a huge dance floor with tables and chairs all around. When it was time for the show, the floor would rise up to stage height.

The shows were wonderful. Full 18-piece orchestra, dancers and singers. Fabulous and very glamorous for Portland.

Roxy was a dancer in the show. Gracie Hanson was the MC and she was the consummate performer. She would go to Las Vegas, see a Totie Fields show, tape record all the jokes, and then when she got home, she would write them on the back of a big fan so she could read them when she was on stage. We always knew when Gracie had a new routine because she would come on stage with that fan.

The ladies powder room off the Roaring 20s Room was like the inside of a candy box. It was very lovely and had a full-time harpist playing within its pink brocaded walls. Now there is something to put on your resume: Toilet harpist. There were gilded chairs on each toilet so that you indeed were sitting on a throne.

The men's toilet was the ultimate adventure. It had a huge urinal about 12 feet long and 7 feet tall that looked like a rocked-in grotto. Little forest animals sat on rock ledges or stood as if they were on the forest floor. They all had bull's eye targets on them. Now all you men know that when we are standing at a urinal, we only look straight ahead, up or down to see that everything is coming out okay. We never turn our heads from side to side and we NEVER talk. Not so at the Roaring 20s men's room.

"Excuse me, but could you move over? I am trying to hit that bunny."

And if they did hit the bunny, ears would wag, tails would go in circles, and eyes would light up. The grand prize, however, was a life-sized replica of Fidel Castro in the very middle, with his mouth wide open. If gentlemen could hit that open mouth, lights would flash, sirens would go off, and a huge waterfall would come down and flush the entire urinal.

Once a night, Gracie Hanson would tell all the ladies to follow her and yell in the men's room door for the men to clear out. Then she'd take the ladies by the hand and say, "Come on, gals, we're goin' in!"

So there we were at the Hoyt Hotel. Me holding on to Roxy's arm so hard he probably had finger marks. I hobbled into the ball room and there was Gracie Hanson standing at the entrance. She slowly looked me up and down and then said calmly, "Nice outfit, Walter." Roxy had forgotten to tell me that he had not gotten permission to borrow my costume. I think he almost lost his job over that one.

When we walked into the room, it was full of about 200 fabulous-looking people dressed to the nines. I just held my head high and walked into the room feeling like a million bucks. Across the way, I saw my reflection in one of the full-length mirrors. I stopped dead in my tracks, took a good look at myself, and thought:

"WALTER, WHAT THE HELL HAVE YOU DONE?"

CHAPTER 2

Linnton, when it was a town

My parents were married in 1929. Richard Lee Cole was 23, Mary Caroline Rickert was 18. My dad adored my mother and it was truly a love match. I was born in 1930, their only child.

What I remember of those early years was of a couple and their child who didn't have two pennies to rub together but were happy nevertheless. Heck, I thought everyone ate beans seven days a week. We lived in Linnton, now a suburb of Portland, and my father worked at one of the three lumber mills in Linnton at that time and probably made a dollar a day.

Linnton was about nine miles down the Willamette River from downtown Portland, and in those days there was nothing in-between except a shantytown. Just like in the Grapes of Wrath, there were shacks with tin roofs and bonfires all around. It was the end of the Depression and I can remember riding by that place on the streetcar when I was maybe as young as 3.

We were doing better than that. We lived in a "company house" that the mills provided for the men and their families at very low rent. It was the basic of basics. Four rooms: two bedrooms, living room, and kitchen. We had an inside toilet and bath but no central heating. There was a wood-burning circulating heater in the living room and a wood-burning cook stove in the kitchen. Cold water had to be run through the cook stove to get it warmed up, which meant that even in the summer we would have to stoke up the stove if we wanted hot water for a bath in the big claw foot bathtub. Because it was a mill-owned house, it did have wood wainscoting up the walls, but the floors were linoleum and there were green pull-down shades on the windows and one bare light bulb that hung down in the middle of each room.

We had iron beds, not the pretty iron beds; these were like bent two-inch pipes. We put the mattresses right on top of the iron springs. No sofa, we just had a couple of over-stuffed chairs in the living room.

The kitchen was the biggest room in the house. There was the big stove with a hot water tank next to it, a big porcelain utility-type sink, very few cupboards with no counter space to speak of, and a big table where everything was prepared and then we pulled up chairs and ate all our meals there. There was nothing fancy or attractive or even comfortable about any of it, but we didn't know the difference. We were together, it was home, and I don't ever remember being hungry or going "without" anything.

Linnton in those days had one paved street, Highway 30, that still runs from Portland to Astoria. Lined up on both sides of the highway were stores like a little village. On one side of the street we had a garage with a full-service gas station and an Italian grocery store with baskets filled with sausages, cheese, fresh produce, and what have you. It smelled so good when you went in, you couldn't stand it. There was also a dentist on that side of the street, a dry goods store, a little restaurant, and Mrs.

Olson's Red and White Grocery Store, which had racks of charge slips. Everything was charged...we would buy something and it would be written on the slip and then when the men got paid at the mill every two weeks, they would come in and pay their bills. There was no hotel, but there was a rooming house for those who worked at the mill. That was on the side closest to the river.

Also on the riverside of the highway was a shoe repair shop. The shoe repairman's son was the first gay man I had ever seen. He decorated the windows at Newberry's variety store in Portland, a clear sign he was "light in the loafers" even though back then I did not know what that meant.

Linnton Feed and Grain was there and still is in the same old building today. There was a meat market where we also bought ice for our icebox. I would go down into the basement where a man would carve a piece of ice and put it in my wagon. I would pull it home and my dad would lift it into the icebox. My favorite thing was to buy a couple of pounds of weenies for the house, then sneak one out of the package and eat it cold on the way home where no one would be the wiser. During the war we had tokens and coupons for meat, butter, cheese, coffee, etc., but again, I don't remember not being able to get something.

Dr. Brouse, who was the doctor for everyone in town, had an office on the main road and next to it was a really neat pharmacy with a soda fountain.

The winery in town had wine brought right to the back door by train in those big round tank cars. Men would fill up the wine bottles right there from the huge containers. During the war wine was scarce, so people who worked at the winery would go to downtown Portland

and sit in a doorway somewhere with wine bottles in a box and sell it until it was gone. Soon taverns started springing up in Linnton, several taverns. A mill town is never short on customers for taverns. And then of course there was a barbershop and a smoke shop, both of which are still going.

In those days, Linnton seemed to be a place where immigrants would settle. I suppose because of the work in the mill, it was cheaper to live there and because Portland proper might have seemed like too big a place to get started. There were many Italians who lived up on the hill. Not because they were richer, they just stayed removed from the rest of the town. They were the merchants and had the businesses on the highway. We lived down below on the riverside of the highway where lots of Czechoslovakians also lived. Our people all worked in the mills.

There was no movie theater; we had to go to St Johns to go to the movies but the heart of any activities in town was the Linnton Community Center. Every week in the middle of the week, Mr. Prince, who was the pastor of the Methodist Church and director of the center, would run a 16mm movie in the gym. He'd line up chairs and everyone would sit there and watch. On Friday nights they had skating with those old clamp-on roller skates. As a matter of fact, I got a job for a dollar a night, putting skates on people. I even got to blow the whistle once in a while to make folks skate in the other direction. It was the big time. There was a library upstairs that doubled on Sunday as the sanctuary for church services. We could also go to Arts & Crafts a couple of times a week. There were things like painting something on a piece of plywood and then Mr. Prince would cut it out for you. My expertise in the "fine arts" probably started there.

Because everyone in the town was poor, the usual entertainment was pinochle parties with home brew. I hated those parties because if we went to someone else's house, I had to lie down on the couch and it was too loud to sleep. Even at our house I never slept, but at least I was in my own bed. One night, when I was about 3, I went around while the adults were busy playing cards and drank the small amount of sediment out of several bottles. I got very drunk. My mother was furious but my father patted me on the back, proudly saying, "That's my boy."

I was a good boy growing up…probably too good. But then most of the kids were good in those days…except maybe on Halloween. It was a small town and everybody knew everything about everybody. If you did anything wrong, everyone would know, so you pretty much kept your nose clean.

We had a couple of problem families. The Palmer family was really the white trash family. She was a great big lady with about 8 children, who all ran around causing trouble all over town. He worked at the mill and probably was a drunk.

But the classic drunk family was the Cherrys. They lived behind us over the tracks toward the mill and were Czechoslovakian. Their name had probably been changed when they came to this country. I think they had about 3 or 4 children and she made the best blackberry dumplings in the world: a little sugar…a little dough…blackberries…and then boil those things. Oh my God, I can still remember how good they were. I liked the family, they were fun. But Mr. and Mrs. Cherry would go to the tavern every Saturday night, drink themselves silly, stagger down the track going home late at night, and then Sunday morning walk to the Catholic church down the highway like nothing had happened.

We didn't have a car, so my mother would take me into Portland on the streetcar. We would go to a movie and always had pork noodles before making the ride back to Linnton. Old Town in those days was the hub of the Chinese community. All the grocers had produce out on the sidewalk and plucked chickens hanging in the windows. There were gambling dens, restaurants, barbershops, schools, and of course the famous tunnels under the buildings where people had been "shanghaied" onto ships docked at the river. The people spoke Chinese, dressed in Chinese clothes, and lived above the stores. The restaurant where we always went for noodles was called the Manila Café and was across the street from where my club is now. The sign is still on the building.

The movie theaters were uptown where the department stores were. I was mesmerized by all the store windows…mannequins with all the pretty clothes on. At Christmas, all of Meier and Frank's windows were decorated with Christmas scenes like Santa's Workshop or the Night before Christmas with moving parts and music.

Some of the streets were cobblestone with many cars and delivery trucks. The Courthouse was right there next to Meier and Frank and the big beautiful Portland Hotel was where Pioneer Square is today. Going to town was exciting to me. It was always an adventure with lots to look at. It was a world I never dreamed I would someday be part of.

There must have been maybe ten or more movie theaters up and down Broadway, Park, and Stark Streets. One only showed newsreels, another only Westerns. I loved scary movies and then could never sleep. I also loved serials like Tom Mix; Mother would bring me back often so I would not miss an episode. When I was about 9, Mother took me to see Gone with the Wind at the United Artists Movie Theatre. I will never forget just before intermission when Scarlet O'Hara is standing in the middle of the fields covered in dirt holding some sweet potatoes high up in the air while shouting at the stormy sky, "As God is my witness, I will never be hungry again." I was very impressed with that scene and I think somehow it lodged itself in my young brain and became a mantra for me in later years. That was one gutsy woman.

Any other of the memories I have of my childhood in that house are scattered. I remember kid things like my cousin and my young aunt coming to stay and all of us sleeping in the same bed. At night when it was pitch black, I would yell to my mother through the thin walls into my parents' bedroom, "They're making faces at me…they're making faces at me." I had pneumonia in that house and my mother nursed me.

I remember one Easter my cousin and aunt were boiling eggs for Easter eggs and one of them said something to me and I threw a raw egg at her. Boy, did I get in trouble for that one! We had no money and one egg was a valuable commodity and not something to just throw away.

Soon after that, my mother became ill…very ill. I don't really know what was wrong. Back then people didn't discuss those kinds of things, maybe they didn't even know. I think now it had something to do with her heart but then, I only knew that we could not go to town on the streetcar any more…no more movies…no more pork noodles. She just didn't have the energy. Then finally she became bedridden.

I know it was horrible for her to have to stay in bed all the time and not have the strength to take care of us any longer, but for a little boy, it was heaven. I would come home from school and go straight to her room and climb in bed with her. We would talk, tell stories, and laugh. She would get tired and take a nap. I would take a nap with her or go out to play and then come back in for more. I loved it…I had her all to myself and some of my best memories are of that time with the two of us snuggled up in bed.

Since Mother was too weak to get out of bed, her sister Madeline came to stay with us and took care of Mother and my dad and me. She was only ten years older than me, so she was really like a teenage older sister rather than an aunt. We had fun together. I remember going to Newberry's in Portland where we could buy sheet music and Madeline would buy a song book that had all the words to the popular songs in it so then we could sing along with shows on the radio. We grew up together. Now I had two women in my life.

One night after I was asleep, Madeline came running into my room all excited and started shaking me. She was yelling at me to get up. "Run, Walter, run. Go get your dad at the mill…Run as fast as you can!"

I quickly pulled on my pants and without even stopping to put on shoes, I ran up the dirt road over rocks and brambles, across the railroad tracks to where my dad was working that night. The minute he saw me, he knew something was wrong. He didn't even stop to see if I was okay or pick me up to take me back with him. Without a word to me, without even looking at me, he ran right by me down the hill leaving me there in the dark. I cried after him and he yelled over his shoulder. "Run to the fire station, Walter! Tell them it's your mother."

A few minutes later I was coming back down the hill with two men. One fireman was carrying a bag; the other was carrying me because I was barefoot. When we arrived at the house, they went directly into the bedroom. Madeline kept me in the living room. I finally broke away and ran into the bedroom and started to climb up in bed with my mother, like I did every day. One of the firemen gently took me by the shoulder, pulled me away, and said, "Not now, son, your mother just died."

"DIED? Died? Died. My rabbits die, my chickens die. But mommies don't die. Mommies don't die."

My father was standing like a statue on the other side of the room, tears silently running down his face. I ran to him and threw my arms around his legs. He didn't move, didn't touch me, didn't say a word. He didn't even know I was there. He was like a stranger.

Madeline took me into the kitchen and held me on her lap for what seemed like hours. Then I walked into the living room just as two men in suits came and rolled my mother out of the bedroom on a bed with wheels. Madeline said, "That's your mother."

She was in a bag.

"Mama! Mama!"

My mother was in a bag and they took her out the door.

I didn't really know what being dead was, but even at that young age, I understood that my life would never be the same again. I knew on that hot summer's night that I had lost my mother forever and I also knew that I had lost my dad.

CHAPTER 3
Lipstick, lashes, and Barbra

I had a dear friend who was doing some little shows…drag shows… under the name Tina Sandell at a lesbian club called the Magic Gardens in the skid-row area of Portland. This was the late 1960s. There were really no drag shows in town at that time. There were gay bars in the southwest part of town but they did not have entertainment. The only drag anyone could see, unless you went down to San Francisco, was when a traveling show would come to a supper club.

Tina was an excellent performer even back then. Her real name was Jerry Farris and she was a wild person, Native American with long black hair and dressed in costumes all the time so she looked like an Indian woman. As Tina, she would do a show maybe once a week at the Magic Gardens and could do "Proud Mary" better than Tina Turner.

I first met Tina when I bought the Demas Tavern. I opened the doors at 7 AM and Tina with her friend Bamboo would come in after being out all night and "freshen up" in the men's toilet, re-do their make-up, and go back out on the street doing God knows what. She was basically a young lovable kid who drank too much and would take any pill no matter what shape, size, or color that was handed to her. She was part of the Klamath Indian tribe but had not grown up on the reservation. Her mother had many husbands and many children and was a delightful fun person who had an interesting life. Tina was a character, but an extremely loyal friend for 25 years. All the years she worked for us, she was always the consummate professional and fell right into the way we did our shows.

She died in her 50s and probably had 30 more years than she should have had considering the way she treated her body. She lived on hamburgers (she always removed the lettuce and tomato). I don't think she ever had a vegetable in her life and she grew heavy and eventually got diabetes and they started cutting off toes and fingers. On one of her last birthdays, she came into the club (she had long since stopped performing) and sat on a stool and did "Proud Mary." The audience was on its feet screaming and crying…that is how talented she was.

Here's my favorite Tina story: One time she called me up and said a Greek ship was in and they really knew how to have a party and she wanted me to go with her. Bamboo was too drunk to go and Roxy was working at the Hoyt Hotel, so I agreed. We got in drag and she had a taxi come and pick us up at the tavern. It was her, me, and a couple of younger guys. I was in the backseat with the two guys and she was in the front with the cab driver. She leans in to him and we hear her whisper something about a blowjob. The three of us in the back seat just kind of looked around out the windows as if nothing was going on, thinking, Jesus, what is she up to? Sure enough, we get to Pier something or other, we get out, and she stays in the cab, but she is out with us in just a couple of minutes.

I said, "Man, that was quick."

"Well," she said, "I told him to get it ready and I didn't have to do a thing."

We got a free cab ride.

That should have been my first warning.

We got on the ship and yes, there was a big party going on in what was probably the mess hall. There were some women there and we had a couple of drinks and talked and Tina disappeared. Pretty soon, here she comes runnin' with her girdle down around her ankles moving as fast as she can with her little legs just a goin' in a kind of hurried penguin waddle.

"The captain's on the way. Get out. Let's GO! COME ON!"

We ran out of there, down that gangplank, and I said, "Damn you, Tina, don't you ever do this to me again."

We got down on the dock and it was about 3 in the morning by then and we're on Pier One or something. Now what do we do? No cell phones then. How do we get back to town? We were stuck.

Tina said: "Oh, I told him to come back."

And sure enough in about half an hour the cab driver came back and gave us a ride.

I said, "Tina, you got something special going on for you, but when we get back to the club, I am going to strangle you."

That was Tina Sandell. She was a natural talent, a sweet, sweet friend, and one of the best drag performers I have ever seen. God, how I miss her!

One day back in the beginning of our friendship, she said to me.

"Walter, why not come over and do a show with me at the Magic Gardens?"

"What would I do?"

"Lip sync to records in a dress."

" Uhhhhhhhh. Well, okay…sure. But I don't have anything to wear."

Not to worry.

I had done some theater already. Straight theater at Marylhurst College, Firehouse Theatre, Mark Allen Players, and shows with the wonderful director Jerry Leith at Portland Civic Theatre. I was always cast as the Doctor or the Lawyer; then in other shows, I was the Doctor and then another Lawyer. I did Arsenic and Old Lace early on. I played the gentlemen caller, got killed at the top of the show, was hid in a window seat cupboard and had to stay there crunched up for the rest of the show because there was no opening on the backstage side.

I said, "Jerry, can't you cut a hole in the back of this thing because I am dying in there?"

He told me no, because it was a borrowed piece of furniture. By the end of the run, I could have done any part in that play because I listened to it all right there on stage for weeks. They would open the lid of the window seat during the show for some comedy bit and I would always make faces at them.

In one show, I got to play a bumbling husband. It was a show directed by Jerry called Ladies Night Out. The main cast was two couples…me and the actress who played my wife and the actor Tony Giordanno and the actress who played his wife. The premise was that the wives kept going to this ladies only spa and we husbands started to become suspicious about just what was going on in there. So we disguised ourselves as women to get inside and check up on the wives. We wrapped towels around our heads and bodies and sashayed in the place with cold cream all over our faces. Well, of course a lot of silliness ensued as they discovered we were men and we ended the scene with Tony running out the front door and me jumping out the window. When I jumped out the window, my towel would fall off and it appeared that I was nude, but really I was wearing briefs dyed to match the color of my skin.

Now there is a tradition in the theater that on closing night, the actors will do something crazy like change dialog or add bits to make it more fun for them. Jerry forbade the actors to change any of the script sooooo on closing night, the wives are in the spa; Tony and I wrap towels around our heads and bodies and go into the spa after the wives. They find out we are men, Tony runs out the front door, I jump out the window for my exit, my towel drops off as usual, but this night I was not wearing the skin-colored briefs. I was the first documented nude on Portland Civic Theatre stage. And it was my last time on Portland Civic Theatre stage.

When I was in the Army, stationed in Livorno, Italy during the Korean Conflict, I was part of a small theater troupe we put together. We did shows like Charlie's Aunt. No I didn't play the Aunt...I was Charlie and my line throughout the entire play was this: "I would like to introduce my aunt. She's from Brazil...where the nuts come from." That was it.

We wrote a musical about cowboys and Indians (you could say the word Indian back then). I was the medicine man, Chief WaWa. We took the show to Vienna where we performed for the men and their families who were stationed there. We played in an old Viennese opera house with balcony seating in boxes that went up in the fancy interior like a wedding cake. They had a huge circle stage that turned around when they changed scenes by pulling ropes. My big moment in the show was when I stood in front of a big cauldron that had some burning coals in the bottom. I was supposed to have a small handful of some kind of sulfur powder or something that when thrown on the coals would make smoke. One night there I was with my cue coming up...I guess I had a bigger handful of powder than usual and right at the correct moment, I threw it in and pow! A huge cloud of smoke rose up and covered the first six rows. I don't think those people saw any more of the show that night and people on stage were waving their arms around to see where they were going.

So now my theater experience was about to be put to use again on the dance floor stage of the Magic Gardens. Tina got me a long dress from Goodwill and I wore those size 12 petit Springolators and the fishnet hose I had from the Halloween Ball. Wigs in those days were way out of our price range so Tina found an acrylic hat that looked just like the Russian fur hat that Julie Christie wore in Dr. Zhivago. It was white, Tina parted it in the middle, put in a barrette or two, swept it up on one side, and there I was...fabulous!

We stood in a spotlight in the middle of the small dance floor at the club with tables around us. Tina put on the record and I was…BARBRA. Of course, who else would I be?

"People, people who need people…are the luckiest people in the world."

They LOVED me. They clapped and cheered. Wow, it felt great! And I was good at it. I even did a little patter between the only two Barbra songs I knew.

Hey, I think I can do this. I may have found a way to be back in show business.

CHAPTER 4
My guardian angel

Everyone has a guardian angel whether they are aware of it or not. I certainly had one in my life—my Aunt Lil, Lily, my father's sister. She was unmarried and lived with my grandmother in Portland. During the Depression, they sewed clothes for the WPA (Work Progress Administration) started by President Franklin D. Roosevelt to put people to work for hourly wages. She also spent a lot of time at her sister Ruth's vineyard in Napa Valley where she dated a state policeman for a time. She had a nice life being part of a big family who cared for her.

The story was that when I was born, my mother was nursing me but I was still crying all the time and would not sleep. So Grandma and Aunt Lil came to the house, took one look at me and said the kid is hungry, went and got some canned condensed milk, fixed up a bottle, and I slept for 3 days. They saved my life or at least that is what they loved to tell me over and over again.

After my mother died, it was decided that they would give up their apartment in town; Grandma would travel around and live for a few weeks or months at a time with each of her 9 children and their families; and Aunt Lil would come and live with us. She certainly saved my life then. She was my mother, my father, my caregiver, my best friend, and my nurse.

"You look a little peaked today, Walter." Castor oil.

I don't know what it was in those days, but everyone seemed very concerned about bowel movements.

"Did you have a bowel movement today, Walter?" If I said no, milk of magnesia. I learned very fast to always answer "Yes I did" to that question!

My mother's death devastated my father. He was never the same again. He turned to silence, anger, and alcohol. He would come home every night from the mill, eat dinner with us, never saying a word, and then leave to go to one of the many taverns in that mill town. He would come home drunk way after I was asleep. At first I cried, threw tantrums, begged him to stay or take me with him. But it all fell on deaf ears. I needed him so much, but he was just unable to respond, his grief was that deep. I don't even think he knew I was there. So I did the best thing I could have done. I turned to my guardian angel, Aunt Lil.

She was very obese, could not lose weight. Sometimes she would get sick and go to the county hospital up where OHSU is now and they would put her on a strict diet, but it never worked…she just could not lose any weight. So she really did not move around too much but sometimes on a rare occasion we would go out or ride the streetcar into town. On those outings, I was aware of people looking at her and making comments…hurtful comments about her size, not even caring if she heard them. She acted as though nothing had happened, but I heard, I saw, and it angered me and made me very sad for her. I knew that she was the most beautiful person in the world…they only knew what they saw on the outside. It was my first experience with prejudice and I did not like it at all. She made her own clothes but when I got older, I had small jobs doing yard work so I went into a large size dress store and saw a black lace dress and put it on layaway until I could pay for it. I had no idea what size she wore. I just held it up and thought it looked right. I gave it to her on her birthday and she was thrilled. It might have been one of the only store-bought dresses she'd had up to that time. Later, Lane Bryant came along and she could order clothes through their catalog.

Everyone in the neighborhood loved Aunt Lil. Shortly after she came to live in our house, she bought a used upright player piano and everyone would come over and sing along to the songs. Friends would come over during the day and sit on the porch and gossip about the neighbors. The kids in the neighborhood really liked her. I remember her as being a happy popular person and she never made me feel she had given anything up to come and take care of me. I think I probably was her life, just like she was mine.

I went to Linnton Grade School and it was hard…they called me Sissy Boy. I never got picked for dodge ball or baseball or any of the boys' games, but I could hopscotch with the best of them and tear up a jump rope and I was a champion jacks player. Those girls didn't have a chance. To tell you the truth, I really preferred to play with the girls but of course that was all the more reason to get picked on.

My teacher wrote a note home saying that I was severely near sighted and could not see the board. She was right, but after I got glasses, I was no longer just Sissy Boy…now I was Four-eyed Sissy Boy. Thanks, teacher!

Every school has its bullies and ours was no exception. You know how when you think back on your school years and you can't always remember some of the kids' names or even your favorite teacher's name, but you can always remember the bully's name. Bob Palmer. He would wait for me after school and bait me all the way home. There was only one way to walk…no back streets to hide in. He didn't really ever hurt me physically…he just shoved me around and called me names. I didn't even know what they meant. He certainly could get to me emotionally and I would try my darnedest each day to make it home before the tears started.

When I got there, I would run and sit on my Aunt Lil's generous lap, bury my face in those enormous bosoms, and the world would be okay. She was always there.

I loved it when it was our turn for Grandma to stay for a few weeks with us. She was a great woman too and another person in my life who always supported me. She was the epitome of what a grandma should look like. If you called central casting and asked for a grandma, you would get my grandma. Grey hair in tight permed curls. Thick glasses. Wash dress down to her ankles with sleeves to the wrists…beige cotton stockings…black sturdy lace-up shoes and a big apron to cover it all up. She came out of her room every morning dressed and ready for the day. She would get after my aunts because they would still be in their chenille bathrobes drinking coffee. Not her! It was business time. She also wore a corset…stainless steel, I think. I know, because when I would sit on her lap and hug her, it felt like I was hugging a refrigerator.

She would tell me great stories about how she came across the prairie in a covered wagon. I don't think she was that old but if my grandma said she came across the prairie in a covered wagon, then she did.

My Aunt Mag who lived in town and had a car would come out and take Grandma, Aunt Lil, and me on rides. We sometimes would go into Portland and have pork noodles. One day we were driving along near downtown, Aunt Mag and Aunt Lil in the front seat, Grandma and I in the back seat, when we passed a woman standing on the street. My grandmother pointed to her and said, "Look! A whore!"

"Whore, Grandma? Whore? How do you know?" I asked.

"Well, look. Lipstick!" she answered with the voice of God.

"Lipstick, Grandma? Lipstick!" And I pressed my face to the car window to get a better look.

She leaned down and whispered clearly in my ear. "Walter, lipstick is made from prisoners' blood!"

"No! A whore? Lipstick? Prisoner's blood!"

My young mind attempted to make sense of this new adult information. But if my grandma said lipstick was prisoner's blood, and someone was a whore if she wore it, then that was the truth!

Now every night when I get ready for work, I put on that prisoners' blood and it makes me chuckle and think about that wonderful lady.

Grandma and my Guardian Angel Aunt Lil. I still know they are in my life, watching down on me…and I also know they are still there for me no matter what.

CHAPTER 5
Don't tell, don't tell anyone

Over the years, Roxy and I have spoken to lots of school groups from middle school all the way to college. We talk about gay lifestyles, show business, our life and their life if that's what they want to talk about. We answer any question to the best of our ability and tell the truth no matter what it is. We talk honestly and don't sugarcoat anything.

One time we were speaking to a group of middle schoolers at Chapman School in Portland. Chapman is an alternative school for artistic kids and kids who maybe did not fit in well with the regular public school set-up. On that particular afternoon, there were maybe a dozen 9- to 12-year-olds. We were having a question-and-answer period and after a few personal discussions about some subjects that had been asked, one boy in the back raised his hand and in a loud voice shouted out, "I was sexually abused by my father!"

I was stunned. I took a couple of steps back. I was completely thrown for a loop and before I even knew what was happening, I found myself moving forward toward the group, raising my hand to that boy and in a loud voice I heard myself say, "So was I."

Where did that come from? I was totally surprised. I couldn't believe I had just said that. The tears started to flood down my face. I had never told anyone that, ever, not even Roxy.

As I have said, the father that I had known as a little boy went away when my mother died. In his place was left a broken, bitter, angry, sad drunk who never spoke a word to me or showed me any kindness at all. He spent every evening after dinner drinking at the tavern seven days a week. We shared a bedroom, because there were only two and Aunt Lil had the front room. When I was in my early teens, he started coming home in the middle of the night and waking me up....

He told me not to tell anyone. EVER. Don't tell. Don't tell.

You see, to me back then, it was not abuse. I was getting attention and what I thought was love from a man who had not even looked in my direction for years. Now he was touching me, kissing me. I welcomed it. I didn't understand how wrong it was. But when that young man raised his hand at Chapman School, it hit me hard...yes, yes, it was abuse. I was abused by my father. It most certainly was wrong and all the memories came rushing back. Don't tell. Don't tell.

I looked that boy straight in the eyes and said, "You just told. You just told me, you just told Roxy, you just told a room full of your friends. You have taken the first step. You have broken the spell...you will be all right. Don't let it make you a victim. You will be all right."

In 1984 my father was in the hospital with severe emphysema. His doctor called and asked me a hard question...he wanted to know that if my father started to go, did I want them to resuscitate him. I hesitated for a moment and he quietly said to me, "Walter, I have never had anyone with this disease thank me for three more months."

That did it. I said, "Yes, let him go."

He then asked me to stop by the nurse's station to tell them in person what I wanted. They would of course have the signed order there, but they are trained to save lives and if a family member tells them in person what their wishes are, it helps when the time comes. I went down to the floor where the lung patients were and no one was around. I noticed a door ajar that said "Employees only." I walked in and there was all the staff… smoking in the break room as all the patients were dying from lung disease down the hall. Is that ironic?

They moved my father to a care center in Gateway and I would go visit him every day usually around mealtime so I could help him eat. We talked about everything…we laughed a lot, but we never talked about or even hinted at "don't tell."

On December 25, 1984, at 7:30 in the morning, I got a call from the care center that my father had passed away. I said thank you and hung up the phone. I felt nothing. It was Christmas… we went on with the day. I was numb. We opened the presents and ate the food as though nothing had happened. I don't know if it was right or wrong, but I could not feel pain, relief, or anything. He was just gone.

After I came out, my father's sister, Aunt Arla, pretty much disowned me. But two weeks after my father died, she sent me a copy of his will in the mail. At the end of the second paragraph it said, "I never fathered a child."

Above: My mother Mary at 16 years of age. A talented seamstress, she made all my clothes and my father's shirts.
Below: My father Richard. A rugged outdoorsman, he worked all his life in the lumber mills of Linnton, Oregon.

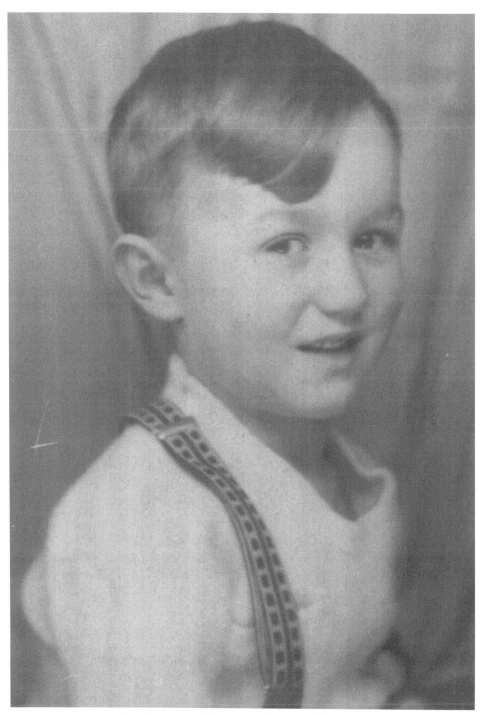

Me, 3 years old, precocious and happy.

Grandma and I out in front of the company house in Linnton, Oregon where my mother died. Grandma travelled around living for weeks at a time with each of her family members after my mother's death.

My guardian angel Aunt Lil' and her boyfriend Charlie at her sister Ruth's vinyard in Napa, California during the Great Depression.

Left: My mother about 2 years before she passed away, pictured here with with her sister Madeline (right).

Right: A playmate and I on Easter Sunday while visiting Aunt Ruth in Berkeley, California.

Left: You should have seen the one that got away!!

Above: The Cole Family Reunion circa 1940.
Below: Aunt Arla, Aunt Mag, and Aunt Lil.

The streets of Linnton, Oregon in the 1930s.

Just Call Me Darcelle 49

Left: Linnton Grade School
Linnton, Oregon

Right: Lincoln High School
Portland, Oregon

Left: US Army, Camp Darby
Livorno, Italy

My first business, Caffe Espresso Coffee House, SW 6th & Harrison, Portland, Oregon

Demas Tavern, 208 NW 3rd Ave, Portland, Oregon. Renamed the Darcelle XV Showplace in 1974. Many changes since then.

The interior of Demas Tavern looking from the front door back to where the stage now stands.

Above: My acting days. I played Augustus Caesar at Marylhust College. Below, some tough guys try to rough me up in a military production of *Charley's Aunt* at Camp Darby in Livorno, Italy.

Left: My daughter Maridee, son Walter Jr., and wife Jean on a family vacation to Disneyland in 1960.

Right: Maridee and Walter Jr. on the Pirate Ship in Disneyland.

Left: The NE Portland home Roxy and I bought in 1978.

Young, handsome, and full of dreams for the future.

Above: Publicity photo of Roc Neuhardt on the California Coast.
Below: Roc (left front) flying high with the Jet Set Review at the Aladdin Hotel in Las Vegas, Nevada.

Just Call Me Darcelle 57

That's me performing on an 8' banquet table doubling as a stage at Demas Tavern. We did two shows a night. Roxy or Tina would put the needle on the record and I would perform while they were changing. When I was finished, I would turn the record over for their performance and run to change my clothes!

Left: My namesake Denise Darcel. We met her in Seattle, Washington when she was appearing in the musical *Follies*.

Right: My dear friend and traveling companion, Bobby Callocotte.

Left: Me, Tina Sandel, and Roxy in the early days at Demas Tavern.

Above: Me and one of my oldest and dearest friends, Rose Empress VI Mame (David Hamilton).
Below: Gracie Hanson and I at the Hoyt Hotel in Portland, Oregon.

Left: Roxy and I dancing.

Right: My first high-drag promotional photo.

Left: Me in full leathers during the 70s. I used to sing "God Bless America" wearing this look. The crowd would go wild!

Above left: Roxy wows the crowd with his roller-skate antics!
Above right: One wild and crazy New Year's Eve.
Below: Roxy and I at the 1971 Rose Court Coronation. I ran for Rose Empress XIV that night but lost. I won the following year becoming Rose Empress XV, which I think has a much nicer ring to it. Don't you agree?

Above: Roxy and I in our Coronation Regalia shortly after my stepping down as Rose Empress XV of The Imperial Sovereign Rose Court.
Below: Roxy and I, in San Francisco, make a toast to the good life!

Now over twice the size of the original Demas Tavern, Darcelle XV Showplace draws audiences from all walks of life for an evening of entertainment, celebration, and maybe a little education.

My wonderful family!
Top left: Granddaughter Sara
Top right: Granddaughter Amanda
Center: Jean, Walter Jr., Amanda, Sara, and Maridee
Lower left: Me and Roxy

Left: My son Walter Cole Jr. and his wife Julie after 26 years of marriage.

Below: My beautiful daughter Maridee and her husband Dennis Woodson on their wedding day.

Above: Me in the dressing room just before a show.
Left: Entertaining the audience with my unique rendition of "Rhinestone Cowboy."
Right: Me and Roxy. The couple that drags together, stays together!

Above: High atop the Wells Fargo Wagon as Grand Marshall of Portland's 2010 Pride Northwest Parade. Left: Roxy and I at the Oregon Convention Center with the winners of our 29th Annual LaFemme Magnifique International Pageant; Adrienne Alexander (left) and Lily Armani (right).

Singing with the Oregon Symphony, Thomas Lauderdale (at the piano) and Storm Large at the Arlene Schnitzer Concert Hall, September 18, 2010. It was truly the highlight of my career.

CHAPTER 6
Luck and urban renewal

You are not going to believe this, but when I was growing up, I was shy. And remember, I was also Four-Eyed Sissy Boy, so I would always sit at the back of the bus where no one was behind me and therefore could make fun of me. If I ever went to a party, I showed up an hour early so that I would not have to walk into a room full of people. Mothers hated me…until I started helping them get things ready. I sat in the back of the classroom and never raised my hand, even if I knew the answer.

But when I got into high school, I realized that if I wanted to make something of myself, if that mantra Scarlet O'Hara had embedded in me as a child was going to come true, I had to snap out of this because we all know that the meek will never inherit the earth. So I started on a personal campaign to change my personality. I would make myself sit up front anywhere I was. I would go up to people and introduce myself and attempt to have a conversation. I became almost chatty in class. At first it was very, very painful…but as with all challenges in our lives, it became easier and I liked how people were responding to me. Soon I became a regular bon vivant…at least on the outside.

I also got my first real job at the Multnomah County Library in downtown Portland. I went to Lincoln High School and after school I would walk the few blocks to the library and work from 3-9 every weekday for 50 cents an hour paid once a month. I worked in "the stacks." People would bring me a slip of paper with the number of a book that was not out on the regular shelves. I would find the book in the dark and dusty back room, climb the ladder, and get it down for the person. Then when they were done, I would climb the ladder and put it back. I became quite the expert on the Dewey Decimal System.

Getting paid once a month was a learning experience for a young man who had never had any money. After work each night, I would walk down the park blocks to Oak to catch the bus back to Linnton. However, between the library and the bus stop was Nick's Coney Island. Hot dogs with everything were 25 cents; add a coke for a nickel and it was perfect for an always-hungry teenage boy. Some of my hard-earned pay could disappear quickly, and by the end of the month, I could be down to my last dollar and if I got some food, I would have no money left for carfare. One night I walked all the way home to Linnton, 9 miles; I got home at 2 in the morning. I was too proud (or shy) to ask the bus driver if I could have a free ride. I know he would have said yes, he saw me every night, but I guess I didn't want to admit that I had not handled my money properly.

My next job during that time was at the Multnomah Athletic Club. I was a page and got to wear a uniform much like the one the boy wore on the old Philip Morris commercials. Pillbox hat, short red jacket with gold epaulets and tight high-waisted trousers, white shirt, and black tie. I looked very snappy in that outfit. It made me feel important.

It was a great job. I made much better money and worked there for the rest of my high school years and even a little beyond. Our responsibility was to take messages to the members. They couldn't have a paging system because some of the members might be there for clandestine reasons and did not want their names blasted all over the building. It was a private club after all. We would discreetly find them in the bar or the steam room or even the rooms upstairs. As an employer, the club was very nice to all of us pages. If there was a late party, they would let us stay. We would go down to the swimming pool. One night we took a bottle of mint vodka from the bar and I got very drunk and sick and to this day, I can't drink any kind of mint drink. I made lots of friends at that job and was very happy there.

During those teen years, I started dating Jeanette Rossini. She lived in a house up on the hill in Linnton where the Italian families lived. I lived down the hill on the other side of the tracks. Jean's mother had also died when she was younger, so she lived with her grandparents. They were from the old country and didn't speak much English. The whole neighborhood called Jeanette's grandmother Grandma Linnton because she always had a pot of something on the stove and would dish you up a bowl if you just set a toe in her door. Sunday dinners were amazing. Italians don't make spaghetti as the main course. No, that's just a side dish alongside the roast beef, eggplant Parmesan, and on and on. Grandma made her own ravioli and spaghetti noodles and all through the year, summer and winter, she had that stove going full blast cooking wonderful things. Even though her English was poor, you could always tell what was on her mind. Sometimes she would rattle off streams of rambunctious Italian and then say "son of bitch." It was pretty clear.

Jean went to Roosevelt High School and had a strict curfew. She was a good Italian Catholic girl after all and 10:00 was the limit. I had bought a 1943 convertible and we could sometimes be very lax about getting home on time after cruising around town. Grandpa would always be on the porch waiting but never said a word. One night we were an hour and a half late and as usual he was waiting on the porch, but this night was different. This night he was holding a shotgun....We were never late again.

I went to Lincoln High School and the four years were coming to an end, so Jean and I became engaged. You see in those days when you graduated from high school, you either went to college if you had the money, or you got married. We got married in 1951 at the First Presbyterian Church downtown. It was a nice wedding with some of the Italian traditions such as guests pinning money on the bride's veil. We had no money and the cash from that veil would pay for our honeymoon trip. I later told Jean she should have gotten a longer veil. After the wedding reception, we grabbed up all the flowers, drove to the cemetery before we even changed our clothes, and put them all on our mothers' graves. We wanted our mothers to celebrate with us on our special day. Then we changed and went to the Republic Chinese Restaurant and had fried shrimp and all the trimmings.

The next day, we took our veil money, hopped in the convertible, and headed south on Hwy 101. We stopped at the Sea Lion Caves, the Redwoods, and a couple of motels along the way. We got as far as Crescent City, California, the honeymoon destination of the world. Driving into the town, I got a speeding ticket...then driving out of the town; I got another...so we decided it was time to go home.

We were married in May and moved into a tiny apartment downtown on SW Lincoln. I was working at Fred Meyer in their sign department. Two months later I got a letter from Uncle Sam: "We want you." I was drafted. It was 1951. I went to the Armory, which is now a lovely theater in Portland, but on that day it was full of about 200 men all standing in their underwear. When it was my turn to be examined, the doctor told me to grab hold of my upper arm and squeeze hard...he was going to take my blood. I had never had blood drawn before and when he got that needle close to my arm, I fainted dead away on the floor. They took me anyway.

By September I had been shipped off to boot camp and then to Livorno, Italy on the Italian Riviera. It was the Korean Conflict...I was in the signal corps. In boot camp I was in the group who learned how to set up communications. I had to climb poles and string wire, just like our electric company linemen do today. I ended up being best in my group, which was amazing since I had hated school. I was supposed to be stationed in Germany, but on the train I got a terrible case of diarrhea and by the time we reached the German camp, I was so week and dehydrated that I ended up in the hospital for two weeks. They were actually playing army there, but I missed all the first part, so they sent me back to Italy.

The camp in Livorno was a tent city then, but they were building the barracks. Because I was the new guy, I had to man the switchboard out in the middle of a field and I was scared shitless. It was the middle of nowhere, all by myself at night for 12 hours in a tent with a generator going for my little light globe. The first night, I was afraid to go out and fill the generator. The MPs came by and thank God I was not asleep, I just told them it was slow and they filled up the generator.

I would call my friends that I had left in Frankfurt to make the time go by. After the barracks were built, they got a regular phone system and they no longer needed me in that job, so I went to records at the headquarters. It was a great gig, five days a week, no weekends; we never had to march or do any soldier stuff. I kept track of records and orders for all the different companies and that meant having to live in the quarters of all the different sections, so I moved around a lot.

The differences in each group were very interesting. For instance, the motor pool soldiers were all black and they treated me like a queen, because I handled all the orders and if they wanted something, they had to go through me. It worked out well, because I was just a little skinny boy from Portland who hadn't really ever talked to black people. Then I got promoted to a recruiting office and sat in the front of headquarters and would sign up the boys that wanted to re-up. They got $600 and I so wanted to tell them not to sign on for more, because they would get a 20-day leave and then have six more years of service. But of course I couldn't. I would just hand them the pen and say sign here.

The two-and-a-half-year Italy duty was a breeze; I mean someone had to keep the Riviera safe. It was hard however to be away from home all that time. I wrote every day. We didn't have email in those days of course and sometimes waiting for that mail to arrive could be agony.

When I finally got home from the army, Jean got pregnant, we needed a bigger place to live, and going full circle we moved into one of the former company houses in Linnton, which was about five houses down from the house I grew up in.

The mill had closed and my father had taken a job in Crescent City and my Aunt Lil had moved down with him. So they were no longer living in Linnton.

Our son Walter was born at the Seventh Day Adventist Hospital while we lived in that house. In those days you couldn't really see the babies except through the nursery glass for about a week; even Jean didn't get to hold him much. But I was thrilled. What a miracle! He was a breech birth and all scarred up and we would say… Oh, he's beautiful…or will be. Won't he?"

Then it was time to buy a house. We went out to SE Portland to a new development where they were building tract houses in an empty field. It was out by where Jean's father and stepmother lived. We went to an open house of the model that they had built and decided that that was for us. We got to pick out our piece of land and floor plan and help decide what went in it. Three bedrooms, two bathrooms, full basement, fireplace up and down, and a circulating furnace. I had never lived in a house with a furnace before. Hardwood floors, 50 x 100 foot lot…$11,500.00… $99.00 a month. My hand was shaking when I signed those papers… I never thought I would ever see that kind of money in my life.

Our daughter Maridee was born two years later. We were the typical American family in the suburbs. Dad went to work each day, Mom stayed home, and the kids went to school. We went camping and had trips to the beach. I was even the Girl Scout leader. To this day, women come up to me and tell me they still have the great Christmas decorations that their daughters made in that troop. I thought, at that time, that this was going to be my life and I was very happy.

After the service, I had gone back to work for Fred Meyer, this time starting as a box boy and quickly moving myself up to management. Soon with Scarlet O'Hara whispering in my ear, I knew that I wanted a better life than being a Fred Meyer employee, especially when I was giving out checks to the union checkers that were more than my salary. I had $5,000 from my time in the service and decided I needed to find something that could be mine. I had had an idea brewing in the back of my mind for some time to maybe open a hamburger stand shaped like a pirate ship. We had taken the kids to Disneyland and Walter had seen a motel that looked like a pirate ship and we had to stay there. So I knew the pirate theme would be popular with kids and no one to this day has done a place like that. I opened up the classified section of the Oregonian, looked under business opportunities, and found a coffee house for sale on SW Sixth and Harrison. Not a hamburger place, but the price was right and it was a place to start. I called the real estate office, got the address, and went over to see it.

It was probably a 100-year-old building that at one time had been a drugstore. It was only a couple of blocks from where Lincoln High was in those days and we used to go there from school to have a coke or lunch and smoke cigarettes. Now as the coffee house space, it had three rooms. A main room when you first came in, half a counter that came to a door that led to a small room that was the kitchen, which was only big enough to wash dishes and make sandwiches. The front room had wooden chairs and wooden tables and in the back was a bigger room that had small tables and wrought iron chairs like a sidewalk café; it served as a gallery for art.

Now I had no idea what I was getting myself into and that may be the secret of success, at least for me. I liked the building, the rooms, and the shutters on the front windows. It was called Caffé Espresso and it was $5,000, which was all I had. My uncle was a CPA and I had asked him what he thought.

"Well, Walter, buy a pound of coffee, brew it up, sell it, and buy two pounds the next day."

I was a young man from southeast Portland with thick glasses, a crew cut, buttoned up shirt and tie, carrying a brief case. I bought the place. I found out later that the reason it was so cheap and they took the first offer was because there had been a shooting a few weeks before and the guy had to get out of the business because he was stealing or selling drugs or something. Dumb old me. Honest Abe. What did I know about that stuff?

It already had customers. Yes, it was full of hippies, beatniks, and intellectuals. They were mostly nice, easygoing people who smoked a lot of pot (not in the coffee house) and to this day, patchouli oil is not my favorite fragrance because the place reeked of it…but I made enough of the strong espresso that the smell took care of it. The art on the walls was all abstract, and there was a small stage where they read poetry, played zithers, harmonicas, and folk music 6 nights a week. If I never hear Joan Baez again, it will be too soon.

So here I was a business owner making it work one pound of coffee at a time. I also had pizza and made sandwiches…real ham sandwiches and reubens in the pizza oven. I would take the pizza tray, put three slices of rye bread, the pastrami, the sauce and sauerkraut on and zap it. They were so drippy and good you needed 10 napkins to eat one. The place had the only steam-powered espresso machine north of San Francisco, which I very quickly learned to use. It was beautiful, brass with a big eagle on the top, a big boiler with the flame going all the time, and a gauge on the side you had to keep your eye on so it wouldn't blow up. Today it would not be legal. I had tiny little white porcelain cups and saucers that went missing by the dozens. But it was the real deal, very European, the only place in town that served it and I charged $.50 a cup, which was outrageous in those days. But they paid it.

I also found a non-alcoholic wine that Lemma Winery had and I served that and Italian sodas. It was all very continental and exotic. No one in town knew what a latte was. But they caught on quickly. I got little teapots to put the hot milk in and let them pour that into their coffee. I also started doing flavors, like chocolate with peppermint, where I would put a peppermint stick in the cup. You know, if I had kept that place, I would probably be "DarcelleBucks" by now.

At first, I had no idea what I was doing, but I just plowed through and business was booming. I got a piano and quickly added jazz to the mix of music. I hired Mabel, a wonderful black lady from northeast Portland who could play a mean jazz piano. She had huge dangling earrings that she called her hotel earrings because she said she wore them when she played at hotels. They were so heavy that the holes in her ears were all stretched out. They would swing up a storm when she played; I'm surprised she didn't knock herself out. She was there only a couple of days before she said to me, "Walter, in the summer, I likes me a little gin."

"Well, this is a coffee house, Mabel, we don't have alcohol."

"Walter, in the summer, I likes me a little gin."

The next evening, she had gin in her coffee cup.

I also had some bigger jazz groups come in for great jazz on the weekends. Some names would stop by and it was a very hip place, the only one like it at that time, by which I mean younger people could come because we weren't a bar. Tom Grant came and played when he was in high school. The musicians would draw people and finally on Friday and Saturday nights, I had to charge a dollar at the door and give them two tickets for coffee or they would have sat there all night and not bought anything. I would put up people's art but was picky about what pieces I chose and it would sell.

I was still working at Fred Meyer during this time. With a family and a mortgage payment, I still did not feel secure enough to leave the day job. My days went like this. I changed my Fred Meyer job from manager to order clerk so that I could work 7am until 3pm. Then I would go home, take a quick nap, and open the coffee house at 5… work until around 1…go home and do it all over again. On the weekends Jean would help.

Business was going real well, word got around, and we were full most nights. Then I got a letter in the mail, from Urban Renewal. You have 30 days to vacate the premises; here is a check for $5,000. So I found another location on 3rd and Clay right behind what was then the Civic Auditorium (now the Keller) and Caffé Espresso moved.

The new space was five times larger. It had been a tavern and it was very nice. It had three exits and much more capacity for tables. There were stairs to the basement level on one side and the basement had its own entrance. I brought the shutters over from the other location and we covered up the front windows, which made a nice backdrop for the stage and which now could be much bigger. The room was a U-shape with a short wall in the middle where the bar was. I put the espresso machine on the bar right out in front, and all the tables and chairs from the other space filled up the room. There were very nice tiled toilets in the back…I wish I had them now. The stage was in the center so that it could be viewed from both sides of the room. It was a harder room to work because if I was behind the bar, I couldn't see what was happening on the other side of that short wall. I always had a waitress, however, and she worked the whole room.

I got robbed there once or at least a guy tried to rob me. It was a very busy night and a man came in with a big Hawaiian straw hat on and a loud Hawaiian shirt. He pointed the pocket of his jacket at me and said, "Put all your money in a paper bag. This is a holdup." I turned around and ran out from behind the bar onto the floor with a pile of menus and started handing them out and whispering to the people to call the police. Those people never needed a menu in their life, but I was going, "Call the police. Call the police." He was not going to steal my money, I worked too hard.

He figured out his plan was not going to fly and was gone by the time the cops got there. The cops told me that it is a trick to wear a bright shirt and funny hat because you would look at those and never remember his face. (There's a little tip if times ever get tough and you need to be a robber for a while.) I was so scared, I had to do laundry after that. When I turned my back on him, I thought I was a goner. The guy probably gave up being a robber because he had lost his touch.

Now that the place was bigger and closer to Portland State, we had college and high school kids coming in. I kept some of the hippies and beatniks around for atmosphere…I would give them free coffee. With a bigger stage, I could have bigger jazz groups and teenagers would come in with their garage bands. It didn't look as foreboding as the original space so we filled it up with new clientele.

In the basement was an empty space that had been a restaurant at one time and for a while, my director friend Jerry Leith used it for a little theater. He built a stage and fixed it up some. Bob Hicks, the reviewer then for the *Oregonian* called it "dank" but maybe that added to the atmosphere. Then Jerry rented a space next door that was bigger, and it was at that location that I did my first play with Jerry, No Exit. That show seemed to draw every nun from St. Mary's, which was just up the street. There they all were nightly in their habits waiting for us to die and go to hell.

The basement there was basically just one room with a kitchen and a couple of restrooms. After Jerry moved next door, I decided I would use the space. I didn't really have to do much to it; we used a lot of black paint and the lighting was not very good, which gave it that smoky Greenwich Village basement vibe, perfect for a jazz club. So it became an after-hours jazz club called Studio A. Any musicians who played around town or were visiting Portland would come and jam after their regular gigs. We had some of the biggest names in jazz play at that club…Cal Tjader, Buddy Rich, to name a couple. They would be in town for a concert or to work at the Candlelight Room and they would come over to Studio A after the bars closed and jam all night. I would cook breakfast for anyone who was still there at 5 am.

Pretty soon it became apparent that I had to quit working at Fred Meyer. But just to be sure I had enough money coming in, I opened an ice cream parlor on 12th and Montgomery called Café Trieste and hired someone else to run it. It was an empty room with one toilet in a little tiny storage room and no back door. I had a few tables left over from the first Caffé Espresso location that I placed around. It was all red and gold, red carpet and gold frames on the walls that I put red velvet in and then took little gold letters and did all the pricing in the frames. Man, what a chore! They hung above the soda fountain. We had sandwiches, coffee but not espresso, and the best ice cream sundaes in town because if you ate the topping off the top of a sundae, I would come along and top it all up again. My clientele was my hippy friends who lived in Goose Hollow who would come by and lots of college kids. It was actually after I opened up Caffé Trieste that Fred Meyer fired me. They felt that because I was selling sandwiches, I was now in competition with their Eve's Kitchen…brother!

My empire was moving right along. I was working very hard and loved it. I don't know where this all came from—how I thought I could run my own business, cook the food, make the coffee, hire the musicians, but probably it was from the desire to not live in a little house with linoleum on the floor and no central heating. If I had had a better childhood in a better house, I don't know if the drive to succeed would have been as strong in me.

Then one night an executive from KOIN, whom I rented the Caffé Espresso space from, came in with two bodyguards. I don't know what he thought he was going to find or what I might do, but he handed me a letter from Urban Renewal. I had 90 days to vacate the premises and here is a check for $5,000.

So I put all my equipment in my garage, fired the manager at Caffé Trieste, and just ran the place by myself. That lasted about 6 months and I got a letter in the mail from Urban Renewal. I had 30 days to vacate and here was a check for $5,000. So once again I looked in the classified section of the Oregonian under business opportunities and found a tavern in NW Portland on 3rd and Davis right in the middle of what we then called skid row.

It was called the Demas Tavern, owned by a Greek family, and Mr. Demas wanted to sell the place and move back to Greece. Mr. Demas was a character who had had the tavern at that location for probably 50 years. He would pretend he could not speak English until something came up where he could maybe earn ten cents instead of five and then he understood perfectly well. I contacted the real estate office, got the key and the address, and went down to see the place. After stepping over a couple of passed-out drunks in the doorway, I stepped inside. Oh my God, I thought, Walter, what are you thinking?

The place was a mess. It was a long deep room (half the size it is today) with an old carved bar down one wall, some shabby-looking booths along the other wall, and some rickety tables and chairs in the middle. There was an old oil heater in the corner that didn't work; that was where the winos would hide their wine bottles that Mr. Demas had illegally sold to them because he only had a beer license. When the cops would come in the door, you would hear clank clank as those bottles disappeared into the stove.

What can I say? I bought it. Bill Naito owned the building and when I told him I was buying the tavern, he said, "Good, that will be great. Why not rent the space next door too?

It was an abandoned skid-row restaurant and he said I could rent both spaces together for $200 a month.

"But there is no opening between the two rooms," I said to him. "Will you put in a door?"

"No", he said, "if I put in a door, I'll have to get a permit…you put in the door and no one will know."

Bill Naito was the nicest landlord. He charged me that $200 rent for 15 years. Over the years he would see me on the street and ask "Walter, are you still doing the masquerade?"

So I put in the door and put a couple of pool tables in there and opened up for business. I had one glaring problem however: no customers. Or let me put it this way, the customers I did have were passed out by eight in the morning.

My idea to open a gay bar was not going too far either because all my gay friends told me they would never come over from the SW side of Burnside no matter what I had going on over on the NW side. What to do? Well, I knew a great lady bartender who often came into Caffé Espresso. Her name was Papa Scott. She was a lesbian lady…or more accurately she was a dyke. An old school dyke who wore men's suits and ties, had a crew cut, bound her breasts, and even wore men's underwear or so she told me…I never checked. She had a heart as big as she was and she said she would come and work for me. She did and we opened the doors and customers streamed in. Female customers…we were now officially a lesbian tavern.

Now, this was many years ago and when I say lesbian, I am not talking about the attractive, well-mannered, kind, lesbians we have today… No, I'm talking about hard-core, militant dykes. The kind you do not want to mess around with. These ladies were angry… ANGRY! We only served beer and wine and right away it became clear that glass pitchers of beer were not going to work. If a lipstick lesbian came through the door to meet her girlfriend and just happened to stop to chat with another girl along the way, a glass pitcher would fly across the room and very possibly knock the poor unsuspecting chatterer out cold on the floor. We changed to plastic pitchers. Glass ashtrays also had to go, as they made big dents in the walls and in heads…we switched to tuna cans. It was a classy joint.

I learned my club negotiation skills in those early days. I quickly over came my gentlemanly ways and thought nothing of picking up a woman and tossing her out the door on her ear. I would get tearful phone calls the next day asking to come back…I didn't always say yes right away. Those women helped me learn the bar business from the bottom up. God bless them.

When I first bought the tavern, the buildings across the street were no longer Chinese businesses and living quarters. Now Gypsies lived there, real Gypsies like you see in pictures. The women wore colorful shawls and skirts to the ground and lots of jewelry. The kids would play in the street. They were clannish so they stayed to themselves unless they were going to have a big celebration and then they would come over to buy kegs of beer. The queen of the Gypsies lived over there and so there was a lot of company. When she died, her body lay in state. It was summer and very hot so the door was open and you could just see her in the room…and days and nights for almost two weeks she lay there in that heat while Gypsies from all of the United States came to pay their respects. Then on her funeral day they put her in a hearse and all the people walked behind it to Rose City Cemetery on the other side of town. They wailed and carried on. The very next day the buildings were empty…they all just disappeared in the middle of the night and moved out to 82nd Street.

The laws in the early days made it so taverns had to close at 1 am and we could not have any kind of entertainment other than a jukebox. Even singing "Happy Birthday" to a customer was against the rules. But in a few years OLCC rules started to lighten up and we could have a singing and performing under certain circumstances. So I called Tina, who was still doing shows at the Magic Gardens, and asked if she would like to come over to my club and we could put together something for a couple of nights a week.

We didn't have a stage so at one end of the room we set up two long banquet tables that stuck out like a runway. We hung a curtain to block off a back storage area as a makeshift dressing room and back stage. I had no sound equipment at all and knew nothing about it so I went to a hi-fi stereo store like you would go to buy a system for your home. I told the man what I needed and he just started putting boxes of the various components on the counter.

"No, no," I said. "You don't understand. I know nothing about this…I need you to plug them all together."

It took five of us together to carry all the plugged together pieces to the van and then five of us to take it into the club so that nothing would come unplugged. Because if it did, I would not know how to plug it back together. I told the man to give me long cords because I didn't know where I was going to put it. I bought an old display case, put it in our makeshift backstage, and we put the turntable and the guts of the system into that case and ran the speakers out to the audience and put them on tables.

We had no lights except one spotlight. Well, it wasn't exactly a spotlight. It was a slide projector, which I would set on the popcorn machine that was by the front door, and whoever might be sitting close by that night became the operator. The tricky thing about slide projectors, however, was that if you tipped them even the slightest one way or the other, the light would go out. So the spotlight on the performer could depend on the level of intoxication of the night's chosen operator. Many a show, I finished singing "People" in the dark.

We didn't really have costumes then. They were just women's street clothes. So I started making one costume a week. I will say they weren't very glitzy, but I tried to have a change of wardrobe as we changed the show. The first thing I ever made was a pair of white leather pants.

Roxy said, "Are you sure?"

"Sure," I said. "How hard can it be?" I just laid out a pair of jeans and used that as the pattern. I still have them but of course it has been a very, very long time since they fit me.

When we first started doing these shows at the tavern, we kept the costumes in the basement just like today, but in those days there was only a trap door to get down and up and when the place was open with people sitting at tables, we couldn't open the trap door. Before the tavern opened, we would gather up all our stuff from the basement and hang it on a make shift rack in our tiny back stage. There was hardly room to turn around, let alone change clothes, and sometimes we came out from behind that drape looking very strange, with a dress on inside out or a wire hanger dangling from our hem.

Tina did "Proud Mary" and I did Barbra. I could do two shows… Side A and Side B. It would go like this….One of us would take care of the record while the other one performed. The needle would be dropped on the record usually starting with that scratchy sound. We would step out from behind the curtain, walk out on the banquet table, and then lip sync and dance a little. If we were lucky, the light would stay on and we would not fall off.

I also had to talk. I mean we were up there, we had to do something especially if the record didn't work or that light went out. I had to talk a lot. The lesbians LOVED it. They went crazy and we loved doing it. I don't know a better way of learning a craft. I don't see how you can get good if it is all handed to you and everything is perfect. You need to learn on your feet. Those ladies were a tough crowd at first but once we got up there in a dress, they were totally with us.

Soon after we started the shows, the Hoyt Hotel closed so Roxy came over to do shows with us. He had been a dancer at the Hoyt Hotel and before that Las Vegas and other points. He was very professional and good at what he did. So the first night he was at our club, there he was with his suit, his tap shoes, and his music. He went out there and tapped his heart out and there was one clap. So as in show business tradition, we blamed the audience…it was just a bad night…and the next night he went out there again. Suit, tap shoes, music, and tapped his heart out and…silence. So in his infinite wisdom, he said, "You know, I don't think those women want to see a man on stage."

The next night, he put on a curly red wig, a tutu, and makeup. He went out there with the same tap shoes, the same music, and brought down the house. They had never seen a drag queen tap dance before. Later on he graduated to doing a number on roller skates on that banquet table and he never fell off. He sent the crowds into spasms of delight every time.

Business was good and we needed more space for seating. It was time for the wall to come down between the two rooms. So for several months every night after the tavern closed, Roxy and I plus any employee who was willing to stay would chip away at the plaster and wood, fill up those big green garbage bags and leave them in other people's dumpsters all over town. We never closed the club and the wall came down.

We put in more tables and chairs for the growing audience and as the laws kept changing, we kept doing a bigger and bigger show. One night a reporter from the Willamette Week came in, Susan Stanley. She wrote an article about the "best-kept secret in Portland" and they came… they came across Burnside…they came from the gay community…they came from the straight community…they came and filled up the room and we were off and running. That was the beginning. Learning the business bit by bit.

I kept the name of the Tavern Demas until 1974 when I stepped down from my year as Empress. It was New Year's Eve and we had a 100-hour weekend. We started on Friday night and New Year's Eve was on Sunday. We stayed open 24 hours a day and had shows every hour. People came all night and all day. That's when we changed the name to DarcelleXV.

There is one other business we had during the time when we were first doing shows at the tavern. I went out one Mother's Day to help a friend who later bought Erv Lind Florists. At that time, they had a shop in Oregon City with flowers and a little candy store. I enjoyed it and I thought, Now this is just fun.

So I talked to Mr. Naito about an empty space on the corner of NW Second and Burnside and told him we wanted to start Old Town Flowers. He rented it to us cheap. In part of it, I put in a little sandwich shop, which I leased out. We had a little red and white candy shop, a huge plant area with a big 4-tiered fountain, flowers of course, and we also sold a little jewelry.

I hired Miss Terri, who was a great designer, and Roxy was the delivery person. We would get up in the morning after working late into the night. We had a Suburban and we would go to the flower market and the shop and haul all the stuff around and we had a great time…for the first year. But after the first Christmas rolled around and the first Mother's Day when you do 8,000 little bouquets that had been ordered through Tele-Florist or whomever. We would use their containers and of course they took their part right off the top and we would say, "We should have made more money than that…we worked ourselves into a coma."

Then we started making fruit baskets and delivering them for holidays. One time Roxy delivered this big $100 basket to a retirement home in NW Portland. Someone back east had ordered it for her mother. When the woman answered the door, she took one look at Roxy and then the fruit basket and started.

"Why the fuck did she send me a fruit basket? What am I going to do with that? Why didn't she just send me the money? There are 5 bananas in there. I can't eat all those bananas."

Roxy stood there for five minutes, taking her abuse, and he finally said, "Hey I know nothing about it. I am just delivering it to you. Take the damn thing!"

We did a very good business in indoor plants. But they had to be watered and taken care of every day. One time we bought a whole bunch of big philodendrons. They were beautiful and then every one of them was returned because of bugs and we had to refund all the money. That's the way it would go. So finally after over three years of working all night and then working all day, we sold it to Dick Calhoun, who stayed at that location for some time and then moved somewhere else in northwest Portland. The best part of that business was going to the gift shows in New York. We still have lots of things around our house that didn't sell so when we sold the business, we brought it all home.

When I was working at that Fred Meyer sign shop, I certainly never set out to have coffee shops, ice cream parlors, flower shops, and especially a drag club in Old Town Portland. I never had a plan of any kind and over the years it has sometimes been a wild roller coaster ride. So much of my success in business has been by chance, the ability to take a risk, the ghost of Scarlet O'Hara, never giving up and just plain not knowing any better. Thanks to an independent spirit and Urban Renewal, life just happened to me and it's been good.

CHAPTER 7
There comes a time

There comes a time in everyone's life when we have to face the truth about ourselves. No more lying, no more cheating, no more not living as my true self. Sissy Boy would no longer cut it. I had to admit that I was queer, a faggot, gay. I had to admit that I was a homosexual. I had to tell Jean.

I was a married man and as I said before, I was happy with that life. Everybody got married; that was what you did in those days and I was just following the rules.

I don't know when the switch was pulled. I don't remember waking up and saying I'm gay. I think it was that I started cheating…with men and I couldn't stand being a cheater and all the lying that goes along with that. I was totally in the closet about it, but I started staying out late, the bar would close at 2, and I would get home at 4. Jean did not confront me on it. I think she thought I had a girlfriend, but sometimes when I got home, she would be up and it got very sticky around the house.

I loved Jean very much and still do to this day. I never fell out of love with her; it's just that the attraction was there and the life I was living became the wrong life for me. I chose the accepted path, it was not working for me, and I had to make some changes. I grew un-happy and I could not live with the deceit.

So finally one Sunday, I sat her down and said, "Look, there is no other woman…I am queer."

I went too far in telling her, by going on and on about how I liked men and what I liked about them but I had to be tough about it so that she would understand. This was like a foreign language to her and I wanted her to know that I was serious. She asked if I was going to move out and I said I don't think so and I'd like to be there a while. Even if it had been other women in my life, it was the deceit that got me. I was not being honest with Jean or myself.

"Why didn't you tell me years ago?" she asked.

"I honestly didn't think I needed to. I didn't expect it to go this far."

I had not had a normal childhood. I knew that the kind of things I was doing were never supposed to be talked about (don't tell) and I really did think that everyone had experienced that in one form or another.

I loved my kids and that was the hardest part, that I would be deserting them, like my father had deserted me. I couldn't imagine doing to my children what my father had done to me, so maybe there was a fear that if I got in a situation, I might be capable of it, so I just walked away. I might have been justifying my behavior to myself…I still don't know. I had been married a long time: Walter was 12 and Meridee was 10.

Unfortunately the kids overheard Jean talking on the phone to someone about it and that was how they found out. I was such a coward, I probably couldn't have told them myself.

My own relatives just disappeared. I was shunned and they would no longer talk to me. My Aunt Arla threatened that if I ever came to her house, she would call the police. That hurt a lot. I had been close to her and after her husband left her, I would stop by often to help her around the house. But after the truth came out, she changed and her negative personality was very persuasive to the rest of the family.

One day my father came into the tavern where I was tending bar in the morning and said he was going to beat me up. Can you imagine the nerve of that man? I just calmly told him not to try it. I had been in the bar business for a while and knew how to handle myself. No more little sissy boy that he could just abuse any way he wanted to.

It took many years to get back with my family. When Walter Jr. was young, he would come with me to the Caffé Trieste once in a while, sweep for me for about 15 minutes, gorge on ice cream, and then go down the street to Powell's Books. It was a great thing to him that his father had an ice cream parlor and I think he bragged about it a little to his friends. Then after I moved away, he worked for Roxy at a club where Roxy was producing shows for the owner. Walter was around 16 then and ran the sound on the weekends. What a treat and education he had there! The shows were nudie girl shows. I don't think his friends believed him when he said he worked at the notorious Sonny's Club. I would pick him up after the clubs closed, I had washed off my face, and we would go to the Hoyt Hotel coffee shop. He didn't know that I was performing in drag. Soon, however, I started getting my picture in the paper in costume with the name Walter Cole underneath and so my kids found out what I was doing. I don't know what they thought... probably that Dad was doing another crazy thing.

I regret those years that I wasn't at this or that, but I couldn't show up to events with Roxy or loaded with jewelry. That would have caused too much pain for the kids. I went to the Father/Daughter banquet and special things like that as a father, but there was that time between their adolescence and adulthood that I missed so much of and you can't get that back.

One time Roxy and I were walking from the club to Saturday Market and we saw Jean and Meridee walking along. This was the first time the two of them had met Roxy so it was awkward for a few minutes, but it opened the door and soon Roxy would come to Christmas and we started asking them to come on trips with us and eventually we became a family again. It is possible and I recommend that everyone make the effort. Today Jean would rather talk to Roxy than me.

Jean's dad and stepmom were great though out it all. Every time there was something in the paper about Darcelle, Jean's dad would cut it out and save it.

And my granddaughters have been a second chance for me. They are our loves. I was in the room when Sarah was born 25 years ago, and I had her in my arms within three minutes. I will never forget that thrill as long as I live and I still tear up when I think about her looking up at me with those little brown eyes. Amanda will be 21 and both of them are princesses and always will be. Sarah has a way she likes to be treated and if a boyfriend is not measuring up, she tells him to hit the road. Amanda is a wonderful dancer and a pleasure to watch. One of the best times Roxy and I had with them was when we took both girls to New

York for Sarah's 16th birthday. When we told them, they started crying and fell off their chairs. Of course both their mother and grandmother wanted to go, and Amanda piped up and said, "I did not hear your names mentioned."

I said, "Thank you, Amanda, because if you ladies go, then we don't go."

Well, we showed the girls the town. First we flew to New York, then took a taxi to the hotel. They had their own room and the first dinner we had was pizza and cokes on Time Square. The girls had tears in their eyes and said this was the best pizza they had ever had. The truth was it was like cardboard, but they were thrilled. They would walk down the street in front of us and loved that people were looking at them. We went to the costume jewelry mart where I get things for the show every visit and I gave them each a basket and said they could get whatever they wanted. They both came back with one bracelet each in their basket and said that was all they wanted. The Chinese woman who owned the place of course knew me and she said, "Oh, that is some good girls." Because anyone else might have had a whole basket full. They may be princesses but they are sweet and unspoiled.

We went to the theater every day. We went to Carmine's restaurant, FOA Schwartz, Saks, the Statue of Liberty, all the tourist things and finally we took them in a horse- drawn carriage through Central Park to the Tavern on the Green, where the waiter made a huge deal over them telling them they could have anything they wanted, bringing them Shirley Temples and treating them like movie stars. You better believe I tipped that guy big time. I am so grateful to have these girls in my life and they LOVE having Roxy and me in their lives. Who else can go to their grandfather's house and go up to the attic to find feathers and beads?

Back when I told Jean, the climate for coming out was secretive. It was a very small group and people mostly met in bars. The lesbians had my bar, the Magic Garden, and the Lotus Card Room. There were more gay bars for the men, especially in the SW part of downtown. No one was going out on the streets holding hands or kissing in public. Portland had had a thriving gay community in the 1940s and 50s that had started before the turn of the century, until Mayor Dorothy McCullough Lee started a campaign to rid Portland of sin by raiding not only gay establishments but burlesque shows, Chinese gambling dens, prostitutes, bootleggers, and any vice that lingered in the city after the end of World War II. By the late 1960s, Portland's Gay Community was not harassed but we still kept a low profile.

In 1969, the Stonewall riot happened in New York and Portland finally started to organize in a more solid way.

In the early 1960s, a man called Sam Campbell would make robes and sit on a chair in the bars and call himself Queen Samuel. I didn't really know him; he had moved to California by 1967 when I owned the bar, but he was a popular character for years presiding over what he called the Court of Transylvania. Then the Pruitts of Portland arrived on the scene. They were a group of gay friends, who all took the name Pruitt as a sign of solidarity and mainly to have fun. They would come down to the club on Saturday afternoon in a Bentley. They would take off the hood ornament, come in and party the rest of the day. Then around 1966, they started having drag balls. During each ball, a queen would be crowned. They also started raising money for charity at these events and donated money to various nonprofits in town or just people who needed help. Out of these beginnings, the Imperial Sovereign Rose Court of Portland was begun based on a similar group in San Francisco.

In 1971, I ran for Empress. In the beginning history of the drag balls, they did not have an elected empress. When the Pruitts of Portland put on the Hoyt Hotel parties, it was more like Queen for a Day. Anybody in drag could go up, sit in a chair, and be judged. You didn't have to talk or perform or do anything. That was how it was done for winners one through thirteen.

Then Vanessa became number thirteen and she wanted to make it a real court system like they had in other bigger cities. It is no secret that Vanessa and I had a very rocky relationship...she ruled with an iron fist and it was her way or no way. At the same time, she was able to see what structure was needed even though she was so damn pushy about it. I ran for Empress XIV that year and lost. (Can't imagine how that happened!) Tracy St. James won and I'll tell you the difference. Tracy did the little sailor suit costumes, little girl look, pink pinafores, stuff like that and she won them over with all of that cuteness. I, on the other hand, had my eye make-up with the black and the big hair and jewelry...the big look. Vanessa had been more put together and not with a big theme going. So the three of us were as different as can be. Vanessa was morning, Tracy was like spring time, and I was night.

The competition was smashing at the time; we had about eight people running and I was first runner-up. So I lost. And I knew I had lost. I could feel it because Mame, my dear best friend, who had been one of the empresses picked from the stage, didn't call me that day like she did every day and wouldn't really talk to me. I knew she was embarrassed because she hadn't voted for me I could tell she had voted for Tracy and she felt guilty. We stayed downtown in the hotel the night of the coronation, I called Tracy and off the top of my head, I told her I wanted to be her Czarina...something I just made up. We were building the court...so she said, "All right. That sounds like fun."

When we went places, she had her look and I had mine. Back then there were four courts, in Vancouver BC, Seattle, San Francisco, and Portland. And that is where we would travel together. I don't know what people thought about me at that time, making up a job for myself, I just did it all so quick. At that time we didn't have princesses and she needed someone to help her. I certainly didn't know any more than anyone else, but I had some smarts about show business and that is what we were doing.

Then in 1972, I campaigned to be Empress XV. In those days, we campaigned for 8 weeks and were voted on in the bars. Then there was a coronation party. I was crowned in the lobby of the Paramount Theatre (now Arlene Schnitzer Concert Hall). The bank of doors where you come in were all draped and there were chairs there…it was lovely. All the contestants went up in the balcony until they announced who won and I came down those stairs like the Queen of the World. What a moment and it worked out for the best! Fifteen is a much better number on the marquee than fourteen.

Back then we were still figuring out what to do. There were no real rules. Nothing was written down. It was so simple. If we wanted to do something, we just did. But then during my reign, we started having a protocol for coronation and eventually we have become a non-profit corporation with a board of directors and all these complicated rules. Over the years, the Imperial Sovereign Rose Court has raised hundreds of thousands of dollars for scholarships, AIDS-related causes, children's organizations both gay and straight, and just helping all kinds of people in need.

The court system was basically a social organization until Measure Nine hit the state in 1992. For those of you who don't live in Oregon, that was the ballot measure that proposed changing the state constitution to basically make homosexuality against the law and lumping it with pedophilia, sadism, and masochism. It was a terrible, scary time for gay people but it did rally the troops to come out to their families and be more open about their sexuality. Groups were formed such as Basic Rights of Oregon and Campaign for a Hate Free Oregon. So at that time any money raised by the court or any other group went to fight Measure Nine.

It was also the time when AIDS was running rampant through our community. I did so many memorials during that time that I finally had to say no. All my friends were gone and I just couldn't do it anymore. So all I could think about was the millions of dollars we raised that went to the campaign fund that could have been used to help people. Our friends were dying, they had no food, not enough medical treatment, on and on, and there was nothing to help them. But instead we had to dump money into fighting a fool. One of my goals with the club is to be an example to all the people from all over the state who come to see the show that we can laugh and have fun and that we are just folks like you.

Happiness has a lot to do with living your life as you really are. I am so sorry for all the pain I caused the people I loved. I am so sorry for breaking up my little family back then. But I am not sorry that I told the truth. I am not sorry I chose to live my life honestly. It is all anyone can really do. I wouldn't change anything that has happened. Marrying Jean, having children, having a house in SE, having all my crazy businesses, meeting Roxy, doing what I am doing now… any of it. We have to be happy, that is the secret to life. Tell the truth, follow your instincts, be yourself, and just be happy.

CHAPTER 8
My life with Roxy

Where do I start? Well, I guess at the beginning.

The first time I saw Roxy was at a bar called the Dahl and Penne in SW Portland. He was sitting at the bar, facing out into the room. I saw this handsome athletic man with a kind face and a big outgoing smile and I walked right over, put my hand on his knee, and said.

"Hi, I'm Walter Cole. I have a tavern down in the skid row area…the Demas Tavern. What's your name?"

He told me he was Roc Neuhardt and that he worked as a dancer in the show at the Roaring Twenties room at the Hoyt Hotel.

"What time is your show?" I asked.

"Eight o'clock five nights a week."

"Do you have a show tomorrow night?"

He nodded.

"I'll be there," I said.

I know he probably heard that all the time. But I was there. Sitting half-way back, my blond hair shining in a sea of audience heads. When I first talked to him and found out he was in show business, I was impressed because I had been in theater and we had that in common. The show was wonderful and so was he. He did an adagio act, which meant he would throw his partner, some wisp of a girl, up over his head as if she were a feather. Very impressive. He told me later that adagio meant dancing with a partner… I think it meant dancing with very little clothes on. After the show, I sent word backstage asking if he would go to coffee with me. We went to the coffee shop in the hotel and talked for a couple of hours. Then I asked if I could drive him home. When we got there, I said good night, he opened the door, went into his place, and that was that.

The next night, I was back at the show. Same thing…coffee…talking… talking about everything…really becoming good friends. Then the ride home and goodnight. This went on the next night…and the next…and the next…for three months. Roxy did not quite know what to think of me, but I had a plan. It didn't take me long to know that this was the person I wanted to spend the rest of my life with and I knew that a one-night stand or a fling would not accomplish that goal.

Finally one night instead of going for coffee, I invited him to come back to the tavern after it closed. There was a small storage room in the back of the club that had a hide-a-bed in it. I opened up the bed and set some candles around. I had hors d'oeuvres and champagne: Ritz crackers with Cheese Whiz and individual champagne screw top bottles and plastic glasses. You laugh about the Cheese Whiz, but did you know there are seven different flavors, no refrigeration needed, and no shelf-life date? Nothing but the best for Roxy!

What happened next is censored and none of your business…but we moved from that storage room to a three-room apartment on Corbett Street. In about six months, that place was so full of Victorian furniture and doodads that we could hardly walk around. It was time to buy a house.

What we wanted was a Victorian cottage….a bungalow…with maybe 5-6 rooms. A cozy parlor…a kitchen with a nook…a fancy carved cupola or two on the outside. Basically we wanted "my baby and me in my blue heaven." I called a realtor friend of mine and he immediately said he had the perfect place. The next day, there we were on the corner of NE Eighth and Thompson, looking up at a widow's walk at the top of a large Victorian house. When we went inside, the first thing we saw was the most amazing staircase I had ever seen. Carved light oak that curved up into the heavens above. Roxy and I stood frozen in our tracks. We looked at each other and said in unison. "We'll take it!"

We didn't care if the roof leaked, if it had electricity, a foundation, or water. We had to have that staircase.

And it wasn't exactly 5-6 rooms. More like 14 with a full attic and basement and it cost $45,000.

But that was 42 years ago and it has been "my blue heaven" ever since.

We set about making the house our own. First of all it took three months to wire the house. When we bought it, there was one bulb hanging down in each room and we had to get a ladder to turn the switch on or off. We had 36 crystal chandeliers and wall sconces.

In the end we have again filled up our living space with so much

Victorian furniture and things on the walls that there is no room for anything else. Recently someone gave me a small framed drawing of myself. It is currently on the floor leaning against a wall as there is no place to hang it.

Roxy was a man of the world. He grew up in Pocatello, Idaho, and West Yellowstone and had lived in Salt Lake City and worked in Las Vegas. Me, I had hardly been out of Linnton. So we started to travel. One of the first trips we made was to visit all those places where he had lived before.

Pocatello, Idaho, was named for Chief Pocatello, headman of the Shoshone tribe who fought against the settlers during the late 1800s. He and some of his followers eventually converted to Mormonism as a way to get food and supplies for his people. In the early days of Pocatello's history, it had a rough reputation that contrasted sharply with the reputation of the Mormon communities close by in Eastern Idaho. The result was a "Babylon in the middle of Mormon country." Roxy told me that growing up you couldn't walk down the street without bumping into a Mormon. By that time, the town had calmed down, was a railroad town, and the center where Union Pacific repaired all of its boxcars and engines.

Roxy's dad was from the Columbus, Ohio, area. It was the Depression and there was no work, so he joined the Civilian Conservation Corps that were building all the national parks. He was sent to West Yellowstone and that is where he met Roxy's mother. Roxy's grandmother had built and owned the first hotel in West Yellowstone. It was called the Madison Hotel and it is still there. We like to stay there at least one night when we travel to that area. Roxy's parents got married and lived there until Roxy was about 6. Then his dad got a job with Union Pacific and moved the family to Pocatello.

His grandparents were always in the picture. The grandmother was pretty much the grand dame of the area. She came from a wealthy famous family in Montana and her nickname was Doll, which her father called her because she was the prettiest of his children. If anyone wanted to get anything done around West Yellowstone, they first had to pass it by Aunt Doll.

When Roxy started college, he considered studying to be a pharmacist, then a nurse, but his love of movies won out. He had started dancing at the age of 8 and knew he wanted to be an entertainer. He studied for many years with a Japanese woman who had New York training, experience, and degrees. During the war, she had been put in an internment camp in Pocatello with the rest of her family. After the war she decided to stay there and start a school. Roxy's parents could not afford lessons, but his grandparents could and they supported his growing love of show business. He got excellent professional level training, ended up being the star pupil, and when he was older, taught classes there himself.

When he was around 19, his mother saw an ad in the local paper that a studio in Salt Lake was looking for a dance teacher. Roxy got a free pass from his dad, who still worked on the railroad. He stayed with his sister who had gotten married and moved to Salt Lake…and went for the job. He got it and taught tap there for about a year, then opened his own studios…Roc's Dance Shop. In addition to running his schools, he also worked during the day for a store that sold RCA products. He took care of the stock. After about five years, he was fired over a misunderstanding but left that job with $3,000 in his pocket from the employees profit-sharing.

About that time, one of his advanced students went to Las Vegas to dance at the Sands Hotel. A year later she called Roc and asked how fast he could get there because she had a job lined up for him. Roxy was on the first plane. He went through a quick audition and the last hurdle was to be able to fit into the pants of the costume. If he could, he was in the show. He could and he started the next day.

Roxy had many successful years in Vegas. He met and worked with many stars until he came to Portland to work at the Roaring Twenties Room for Gracie Hanson and the rest is history.

Roxy brought a lot of that history to our club. Our shows would not look like they do if it was not for the skills Roxy "brought to the party." When we started the shows, there were three people, Tina, Roxy and, I, and we did three shows a night. Sometimes guest drag performers would come and that was good to fill up the time. I did new material every week and so did Roxy, but after Susan Stanley's article, we needed to do more, so we brought in more people and became a 5-person company, which is what it still is today.

Up until that point, we had not really done any production work and that was when Roxy took over. He picked the music and did the choreography and I would do the costumes. We have been the perfect partnership because I would get ideas once he started working on a number, would run them by him, and we would agree on "Hello Dolly" in a "Dolly" dress or maybe another number would call for sequined military jackets. It meshed together beautifully. Without the right music and movements, the costumes mean nothing and vice versa; without costumes, the music and dance does not work either.

Roxy also changed our makeup. He came from Vegas where he had worked with show girls wearing glamour makeup and eye lashes out to there that worked well under the very bright stage lights. He translated that into US…so that we made sure we had red lips, long lashes, lots of eye shadow so that the audience could see our features. All of this was Roxy's doing and every night he would check us each out and even though we might have thought we looked like a whore or a kewpie doll, we were not the girls next door. Roxy's favorite line was "If I want to go see the girl next door, I'll go next door."

And of course when the faces looked like that, I had to match with sequins and feathers and beads and big jewelry, whatever it took to complete the showgirl look. Hell, I got very good at making a French cut, just zip zip and get it decorated. We showed lots of leg, lots of ass, and we insisted that all the girls wear panty hose.

Roxy also taught a lot of left feet performers to walk in high heels and to dance so that our chorography looked seamless. Roxy is very good at seeing the talent in people and is very good at fine-tuning it. All of these details Roxy took care of and he has held high standards as the director of our shows for all these years. It is a tradition now that if you are a Darcelle showgirl, you're not painted like the streets and it is one of the main reasons we have been successful.

Portland has never seen anything like this, not even on women, and this became and still is our foundation and we still hold up the rules. There have been some parting of the ways over the years, but why change what has worked so well? I truly believe that the partnership of Roxy and Darcelle is what has made our shows what they are. If he hadn't come along, I might still be doing Barbra Side A and Side B in a dress from Goodwill.

So off we went on our first road trip. We got in Roxy's Karman Ghia and drove to Salt Lake City. He took me around the city to all of the studios he had worked at, his studios, where he had lived and on and on. Back then, two gay boys in Mormon country staying in a motel with a soaking tub in the living room was quite the adventure. We had such a good time, we stayed an extra day.

From Salt Lake City we were going to drive up to Nevada to do some gambling. On the way out of town, we passed the Great Salt Lake. Roxy said, "There it is…the Great Salt Lake."

I had never seen it before and was fascinated. "Can we stop and go in it?"

"We shouldn't."

But we did and he was right, we shouldn't have. Never go in a salt lake unless you have a fire hose to wash off the salt when you get out. We had salt in places salt should never even think about being. It was very, very hot and we were very uncomfortable. So we just hopped in Roxy's little car and drove across the searing desert. Immediately after crossing the Nevada border, thank God we spotted a huge casino in the distance. It was like seeing an oasis in the middle of the Sahara. I knew there would be food there and drinks with ice and little umbrellas and air conditioning and soft sheets and a SHOWER. Roxy pulled the car into the big parking lot and we both went for the door handles to get out of the car when we looked at each other and realized we were buck naked and covered in crusty salt.

You have never in your life seen two large men get dressed so fast and in the front seat of a Karman Ghia.

CHAPTER 9
World tours

We were always up for a road trip and if it could be combined with work…all the better.

Our good friend Bobby Callocotte was a very talented entertainer who appeared all over the states. We would do shows with him any time we could arrange it. One time he called us from a club in Lake Charles, Louisiana called Hollywood East. He was doing a show there and since he knew we were coming to New Orleans for Mardi Gras, he suggested he book us in there and we could come a few days early, do the gig, then go back to New Orleans. He also said it was a wonderful way to see the sights and scenery on the two-hour bus ride from New Orleans.

So there we were on a Greyhound bus driving from New Orleans to Lake Charles. Three and a half hours had gone by, we had not gotten to Lake Charles, and the only scenery we had seen was black water full of dead trees. I said to Roxy, "We are on another Bobby adventure."

When we finally arrived, it was after dark. We were picked up at the bus station and brought right to the club because the three of us needed to get ready and do the show. We drove down by the water and the road was dark and spooky-looking.

We drove up and parked in front of a structure. The car lights hit it… and it was a Quonset hut…A Quonset hut! With a sign over the door that says Hollywood East. Where is the palace we were supposed to be playing in? This was it? Bobby, what the hell? Although by that time in our relationship with Bobby, this kind of thing was no big surprise…like I said "another adventure." We had learned a long time ago to just go with it and enjoy the ride.

Once inside, the owner…I think her name was Betty or something…I could never remember…showed us to our dressing room…which was the supply room she had cleaned out and put a table and a couple of chairs in. She pointed to a hornet's nest high up in one corner of the room and said, "Don't worry about the mud daubers. They're asleep and they won't come out"

"Well, Gloria," I asked, "if they are asleep, why don't you just get rid of the nest?"

"They'll come back."

Oh yes, we were in the South.

"You just missed the 'gators," she said.

"GATORS!" I exclaimed with raised eyebrows. "Really? When was that?"

"Last week, it was mating season and they come up out of this bayou behind here and cross the road to the other bayou. The place is really jumpin' when that happens."

"I'll bet… gee, so sorry we missed it." I gave Bobby a look that could kill.

The performance area was a piece of plywood on the floor, one light, and a boom box for our music. But we had a great show. Lake Charles is very near Houston, so lots of friends came over from there and the place was packed.

We went to our motel and the next afternoon, we went back to the club to straighten up. Now that it was light out, I could get a better look at the Quonset hut and its surroundings. As I walked up to the front door, I noticed small holes in the wall just above the door.

"Helen?" I called inside. "What are all these holes out here above the door?"

"Oh… Yeah, those. Bullet holes." She beamed.

"Really, when did that happen?"

"Oh a couple of weeks ago, some good old boys thought they needed to teach us sinners a lesson."

I then looked across the road and in the front yard of the house over there was a giant wooden cross outlined in light bulbs.

"Doris, when they were 'shootin' up the place, did the lights on the cross go on?"

"Yep!"

Well, Quonset hut, mud daubers, gators, good old boys with guns, and a cross that lights up. Bobby had outdone himself on this one.

Oh and by the way, Bobby was dark-skinned and for years he referred to himself as Hawaiian, but lately since it was now fashionable, he called himself Black.

We did a second show that night and filled the place again and everyone had a great time. When it was time to be paid, Myrtle gave each one of us a big bag of coins. Maybe, she had a laundromat somewhere. We didn't even know how much she paid us…but the nickels, dimes, and quarters spent just as easily as paper in New Orleans.

The next morning we had to get up early to catch the bus back to New Orleans. As I am sitting there in my seat waiting for the bus to pull out, I notice that our boxes of costumes were being put in the bottom of another bus.

"Bobby," I said. "Look, our boxes of costumes are being put on that bus."

"It's okay," he said. "They're going back to Portland."

"How can that be?" I asked. "We didn't buy a ticket to Portland."

"Don't need a ticket."

"Yes, we do." I was moving into lecture mode.

"Nope, really, it's okay."

"Why?" I was not letting this go by.

"I slept with the driver of that bus last night."

Bobby Callocotte died about eight years ago of AIDS. On his death certificate under Race, it said Caucasian.

Another "Bobby Adventure" was when he booked us in Vegas. A BIG VEGAS SHOW! Roxy and I were so excited; we thought this was the big time. Yeah, the big time. Well, the club was so far off the strip it was completely dark out there and you were lucky to find the place. It was called the Red Barn…because it really was a red barn. Two shows a night. A show at 8 o'clock and a show at 5 am for when the people working at the casinos got off work.

The dressing room was outside where the beer was kept in a cooler. It was freezing out there because the desert is cold at night even in the summer, so I would go into the walk-in beer cooler to change because it was warmer in there than outside. Back then, my Rhinestone Cowboy chaps were made of shiny vinyl and they would be stiff as a board in the cold. The only way they would bend enough to get them on was in that beer cooler.

The entrance to the stage was to climb up some stairs outside (in high heels) to the hay loft and then you opened a door and there were stairs down to the top of a grand piano. That was the stage… the top of the piano. Roxy did his roller skate routine on that piano. There were cables across the barn from wall to wall to hold the barn walls up in the winds of the desert and at rehearsal, the guy told us, "Whatever you do, DON'T TOUCH THE CABLES!"

So of course, Roxy got up there in his roller skates and grabbed the cable and the entire audience let out a loud gasp as the barn swayed just a little bit from side to side. I screamed over the music, "LET GO OF THE CABLE!"

The guy who ran the barn was very nice but he put us in a motel nearby out in the middle of nowhere and it was a whorehouse. The windows were all covered up with foil and all night long it was in and out, in and out, in room after room. We laughed and laughed. When we were driving home after the last 5 am show, we didn't even take off our makeup, We stopped at a Jack in the Box for something to eat. There were only four of us but we ordered tons of food, I mean, TONS of food. The girl on the order microphone said, "Are you joking with me?"

And I laughingly answered, "NO, I am just not used to talking into a clown's mouth."

Then we drove up to the window to pay and get our food and there we were a car full of men with full make-up on…so she had the last laugh on us.

Another time, we went to Milton Freewater, Oregon, to do a show at a place called the Teepee Café and Lounge. The daughter of the woman who owned the place had seen us in Portland and told her mother to book us. We left Portland after a show about 1:30 in the morning and drove all night and we showed up at 8 in the morning all haggard in jeans and needing a shave. The woman took one look at us and said, "What the hell is going on? I hired you guys?"

To which I replied, "Yes you did. We clean up real good."

We had breakfast and set up for the show. She had gotten us a motel with three rooms, but the people there did not like us because we were queer. After the show that night, we went back to the motel and one of our rooms had a gas leak. The fire trucks showed up, the police showed up, and there we were running out of the rooms half in make-up, half not…we decided they were trying to kill us off.

The Teepee Café and Lounge had low ceilings with wagon wheel chandeliers that were just in our sight line and they had those Casablanca ceiling fans that were just above our heads. Every time I did a big gesture above my head, the audience would scream thinking I was about to lose a hand or some feathers off the top. They didn't have any lights to speak of and certainly no spotlight, so the bouncer had one of those huge police flash lights that used about 20 D batteries and he would use it as a spot for us. The place was sold out…cowboys, fruit pickers, everyone was there. Then after our show, a cowboy band came on stage and the owner wanted us to stay and dance with the customers, which we did until one good old boy who was dancing with me said, "You got any DOPE?"

"No," I said.

He tried again. "Come on. You're from Portland, you must have dope."

I gathered all the girls together and we got the hell out of that place.

That lady called us back the next year. That time she put in some lights and a better sound system. Then it burned down and I don't think it is there any more.

Every small town is a funny story. We have changed in toilets, in kitchens, in the back of the room with a sheet in front of us, on stage, off stage, anywhere. We don't care. If they see something, they see something. That is theater.

Darcelle and Company went on a World Tour. At least that is what we called it. We started in Seattle, and then went to Reno and Las Vegas, and then on to Orange County and back up to San Francisco.

There were six of us: me, Roxy, three showgirls, and a male dancer. We packed up all our costumes, personal bags, and equipment in our Suburban and off we went. On the top of the van was our magic box and some wooden dolls we used in the act. The dolls were made out of flat plywood and were the same size as us with the same costumes. One performer would hook a doll on each side of him and they were rigged so that when we moved our arms or legs, the dolls would move theirs too. It could make four people look like a huge chorus line.

We drove from Vegas to Orange County on the freeway. Speeding along, the car full of the usual loud chatter that a vehicle full of drag queens can produce, when all of a sudden the car went silent. That definitely meant something was wrong. I was driving and I looked in the rear view mirror and there were wooden arms and legs and heads and wigs flying down the freeway behind us. I screamed and started laughing hysterically. The others breathed a sigh of relief and started laughing with me. They were afraid I would be mad because it had been quite a project to make those dolls…but I hated that number. One of the happiest moments of my life was to see those dolls flying off the back of the van and out of my life.

When we arrived at Orange County, the woman who had booked us was too cheap to get us rooms… so I found a Motel Six, pulled the van around back so that they would not see how many of us there were and rented a room. We pulled the mattresses off the bed and arranged enough space for all of us to sleep. Then we went across the street to a Mexican restaurant where we proceeded to eat everything on the menu…everything. Tacos, enchiladas, refried beans, chile rellenos… you name it, we ate it. Coming back to that small room and closing the door with six men sleeping in close quarters, it soon became apparent that we had picked the wrong restaurant.

The next stop on our World Tour was San Francisco. We were performing in a really nice theater with a backstage and dressing rooms. I had no sooner gotten settled into my dressing room than the stage manager came in to tell me that they had had a show there last night and the group lost their snake.

"SNAKE?" I screamed, maybe a little too loud. "How the hell do you lose a snake? What kind of snake?"

"A boa constrictor."

"Boa constrictor? How long?"

"Eight feet."

"How in the hell do you lose an eight-foot boa constrictor?

I looked carefully all around my room.

"Well, it's not in here," I said and closed the door tight.

My dressing room was right across the hall from the heating system. Upon hearing the overture, I opened my door and a 25-foot snake with a head bigger than mine slithered out from under the furnace and was looking at me with what I thought was a hungry look on his face. I screamed so loud, they stopped the overture and I could hear someone in the audience say, "Darcelle found the snake!"

Darcelle also does gigs all alone. People will call me up and pay me to come to someone's birthday party or whatever.

One time I went to the airport for the kitchen manager's birthday. I walked in the kitchen and before I got 10 feet in, I had every security guard in the place following me. I went into the manager's office and tried to talk to him and carry on, and he was not at all interested, but the entire staff of the airport was crammed in there and loved it.

The office staff at a car place on Martin Luther King Blvd hired me to surprise their boss on his birthday. I went into the showroom and they called the boss out. He took one look at me, ran into his office, and locked the door, so I sat on the secretary's desk for a while, she gave me the money, and I went home.

Once I was asked to speak at a Women in Advertising luncheon at the Multnomah Club because the president was stepping down and they told me she would just LOVE it. I walked into the room of women who should know about fun but the outgoing president turned her back on me and so therefore did the rest of the room. I said, "Roxy, get the check!" and I walked out. Thankfully, that is one of the only times that kind of reception happened to me.

When I go to parties like in the big pink US Bank tower or some very corporate atmosphere, I have the most fun riding up the elevator with the guests. The door opens and pow! there I am and they don't know what to do.

No matter what happens, whether it is gators, mud daubers, flying dolls, managers who run away, or snakes…the show must go on. And in high heels.

CHAPTER 10
What's in a name?

One of our best friends over the years was David Hamilton…or Mame as everyone called him. Mame was the most fun, positive person I have ever known. Just like Auntie Mame, the line "Life is a banquet and most poor suckers are starving to death" was also our Mame's words to live by. For years we went to Mardi Gras with Mame each year and had a ball. She was always up for anything and certainly the life of the party.

One day Mame, Roxy, and I were sitting in a big booth at the club having a couple of beers.

"Walter," Mame said, "if you are going to continue to do this drag stuff, you need a name."

Up until then I had been using lots of different names: Madame Demas, Sally Stanford (she was the former San Francisco Madame who later became the mayor of Sausalito), or just plain Walter.

"Regular girls' names are out of the question," Roxy piped up. "You are too big, too jeweled, too haired…I think you look French."

I was still back on the "too big" part but said "Okay, whatever you two think."

Years before, when Roxy had worked in Las Vegas, he performed with a B movie star who had come over from Paris. Her name was Denise Darcel. Denise was out of the question…but Darcel was perfect. They both agreed and then decided to add an extra L and E and Darcelle became my name. The next morning, I had to call Mame up to be reminded what my new name was and how to spell it.

The creation of "Darcelle" was experiment after experiment. I had to learn how to do my make-up for myself. After the first time Roxy did my make-up and it took two hours, I was determined it was not going to take that long or I would forget it. Now I can do it in 10 minutes. My mentor was Gracie Hanson. I wanted to look like her. What she did was what I wanted to do and that was the look I wanted. Sequins on eyelids, lots of feathers, big hair, big jewels, and lots of wise cracks. I started talking and being funny and I don't know where it came from, I certainly was not funny as a child. It surprised me and thrilled me that people would laugh and that they liked to watch me. Now these are the signatures of Darcelle that my fans expect.

After talking to the audience for years, I am very sensitive as to how far I can go but sometimes I get surprised. Lately, however, I have gotten caught up with my bit where I tell the ladies in the front row what great-looking bazooms they have. Women love it but one night I made a comment like I do to a party of middle-aged women who came in and sat around the runway. I pointed to one woman and said, "You have the prettiest ba boom bas I have ever seen."

And she looked like she was going to die. Her friends went white, and then she started laughing. It was her first time out after having a double mastectomy. They didn't know if they should laugh or cry. Afterwards, they told me that it was the best thing that had happened to her. When I said that, she perked right up, and her friends said "Now, she'll be fine."

Then another night that week when I did a song called "Bounce Your Boobies," I pointed to a woman and said, "You're the winner. You didn't have to do anything. They just went round and round."

Then I asked, "Are they real?"

"One of them is!" she answered.

Then in the same week I said to some woman in the audience, "Oh, you're just too perky!"

After the show she came up to me and asked what I meant by "too perky" and I thought I should clean it up a bit so I said, "I meant your personality. You seemed like a perky person."

"Well," she said, "I thought maybe you were talking about these. I just had reconstruction after a double mastectomy."

Three in one week. It can be a challenge some times for Darcelle to "chat" from the stage.

One time a whole row of people over by the wall were not laughing at anything. They just sat there. So I went over, knocked on my mic, and said, "Do you read lips?"

They laughed and said yes.

Darcelle and Walter. Walter and Darcelle. It's almost like I have had a split personality over the years.

In the beginning, the two could not have been more different. Walter could still be that shy hard-working boy from Linnton and Darcelle could say and do anything.

For instance, Walter is afraid of heights and doesn't even like to get on top of a ladder. Darcelle flew in the inaugural flight of the Channel 6 news helicopter over Linnton and then on around Mt. St. Helens with a glass floor like it was nothing. Walter would not have gone near that aircraft. At a fund-raising radio show for Doernbecher Hospital up on the hill, Darcelle challenged the public to donate $250,000 in 25 minutes and he would get the radio host in drag and they would both ride the new OHSU tram down the hill and back up again. They did and they did. Walter can't even look at the tram from the ground.

For a long time when I was out of drag during the day, I was Walter. When I was in drag, I was Darcelle. I remember a story about someone making a lunch date with Darcelle. As she and her friend walked back to their cars, she was going on and on about going to lunch with Darcelle the next day and how they were going to discuss dresses for an upcoming show.

Her friend calmly asked, "You're going to lunch? Well, then honey, you're not going to have lunch with Darcelle. You're going to have lunch with Walter."

"I don't want to have lunch with Walter," she cried. "What does Walter know about dresses?"

And so it has been. But in recent years, the line between the two has gotten thinner. Sometimes, I even forget I'm not in drag and will spew out some greeting that could be taken as very rude. Darcelle can get away with it…Walter just looks like a jerk.

One of the aspects of this life that Darcelle has given to Walter is the many awards and accolades that she has received over the years. I have been very lucky because there was a time when I first started, I would get asked to do fund-raising events like for the Heart Association or the Lung Association and I did them all. And every time I did these appearances there would be 500 people there and yes, it was a way for more people to get to know me and a form of free publicity. But what I also felt at the time was that I was being accepted totally by Portland and this was my way to give back by helping these charities, my way to say thank you. I still do them.

Over the years, I also have gotten lots of recognition from my peers in the gay community. Just recently, I got the Matthew Shepard Award alongside Governor Barbara Roberts, which was a major honor. I am really the most blessed by all of the applause at the shows and the warmth I feel anytime I walk into a room no matter where I go.

I have a favorite story about some friends taking me to dinner and saying they wanted to drive me way out of town to somewhere where no one would know who I was It must have been a two-hour car ride… it was like being in the witness protection program. We got to this nice place and we no sooner sat down when the bar tender comes over with a bar napkin and asks for my autograph. I can't get away and of course I LOVE it.

Then-Mayor Vera Katz gave Darcelle the Spirit of Portland award, which was a thrill. On that same day, the mayor gave the same award to the Royal Rosarians. Pretty good company to be in. It reminded me of an incident that happened a few years before that. The Rosarians called me and said they were touring rose gardens of celebrities in town. Did I have a rose garden? Of course I had a rose garden. So on the Friday before the Rose Parade, they came over to the house and I served champagne and hors d'oeuvres in the dining room (real ones, not Ritz crackers with Cheese Whiz) After I gave them a couple of glasses each, we went out to my deck where I led them to two black plastic pots from Fred Meyer…one red rose and one yellow rose. They didn't miss a beat. They were very serious, looked at the leaves inside and out, smelled the roses, took pictures of me with the roses, and of me with them. We went into the house had another glass of champagne and they left. The next day, Roxy and I were at the start of the parade route and one of the Rosarians came up to me and said, "Darcelle, next time you buy roses, pay more than $4.95 a piece."

Darcelle has given Walter a very interesting life. We ain't at Fred Meyer any more, Toto.

Several years ago I got a letter from the Barnum and Bailey Ringling Brothers Circus. They wanted to know if Darcelle would consider riding an elephant from the train station to the Memorial Coliseum with some other celebrities. Would I! Darcelle jumped at the chance.

I arrived at the train station really done up showgirl style. Fish net stockings, bright orange French-cut leotard, feathers everywhere, and tall, tall hair with a headdress on top. The elephants were brought out of the boxcars and let me tell you, you knew they had been in there for a couple of days…whew. The trainer for my elephant was a tiny brown man who spoke to the elephant in some foreign tongue. He rattled something off and the elephant kneeled down in front of me with its front legs on the ground. Then the trainer nodded at me... I was supposed to step on the elephant's leg with one foot and then with the other leg, hoist myself up and over...was he kidding? Sitting down the elephant still seemed a big as the boxcar she just came out of. So I nodded to the trainer that I needed help...he did not understand anything I was trying to say until I motioned pushing my butt up and he got the picture. Up I went.

It is high up there and there was no saddle and nothing to hang on to except a chain they had around the animal's neck inside a fire hose so that the animal wouldn't get cut by it. I hung on for dear life and away we all went, it was the longest ride of my life. The only thing that saved me was along the way crowds of people would stop and wave and I would put on my best Rose Princess imitation and wave back. About half way there, the trainer stopped the elephants, said something in his best foreign tongue, clapped his hands, and the elephants started dancing. I yelled back at the trainer in my best foreign tongue, "STOP THE GODDAMN DANCING!"

I lost all my fingernails holding on to that chain.

When we arrived at the Memorial Coliseum, I slid off that monster and hobbled over to where Roxy was waiting. "Roxy, I have to go home RIGHT NOW! My butt is bleeding. The hairs on that elephant's back were like razor blades... "Oh, Channel 8? Hello! An interview?...why, of course."

Again I put on my Rose Princess act and holding my butt staggered over to the camera smiling and laughing like I had just gotten out of a Rolls Royce convertible.

"What a wonderful experience!" I told them. "So happy to get the chance to do it. Lucky, lucky me!... Will I do it again? Oh probably not. It is so gauche to do something twice when the first time was such a success."

When I got home, I sat in a bath of Epsom salts and was not able to do Rhinestone Cowboy for three weeks.

Walter would have known better.

So over the years, Walter and Darcelle have gotten closer together so that dress or no dress, now I am mostly the same person.

It took a lot of hard work, money, and balls for a shy little boy from Linnton, Oregon, to become Darcelle and I am very proud of that and I have made a great life for myself. Scarlet O'Hara would approve, I think.

I can't believe I am going to be 80 this year. The main thing is: Where has the time gone? I was driving along the other day and remembered something that happened years ago and realized it had been 30 years. What happens to the time? Did I forget something along the way that I should have been doing? Should I have been doing something more productive or more rewarding financially? Should I have been doing something more to help this one or help that one?

Or even with my own family. What happened to the time between then and now? My kids are in their 50s. What happened to the time? (They were born in the 1950s) What happened to that time spent? And yet everybody plows through it. We plow through every day and every day picks up a week and every week picks up a month and every month picks up a year and the next thing you know, you're 79 years old.

But I have a lot to show for it. I have a wonderful life. And even though I was not a doctor making somebody well, or a lawyer making somebody rich, I chose to be a female impersonator and have cured and helped hundreds and hundreds of people. So you think of your life and you reflect back and you remember the highs and the lows but if there were lows, you pulled yourself out of those lows and you made life what you wanted it to be. Then you don't have to worry about those years in between. Believe me, I didn't miss a thing.

There were no role models to grab hold of when I was growing up. So I can't say I am what I wanted to be when I grew up. Are the circumstances of my life just accidental or are they planned somewhere? I think they are planned because I would never think at 79, or have thought at 69, or 59, or 49 that I would be where I am now: comfortable…happy… with a great partner…with thousands of friends…a family that even through thick and thin still loves and appreciates me…so it doesn't matter if I'm 79.

Not too long ago, a reporter asked me if my one-man show was going to be my swan song. I almost got off the stool and hit him. NO, 'cause I'm not going anywhere and to me, I don't even know what that swan song thing means…because somehow I am still walking, still talking, and still making people laugh.

We just did a show at an Elks club in Long Beach, Washington. There were probably 300 people in that room and all of them were on social security. A guy came up to me before the show and said, "At your age, what the hell are you still doing this shit for?"

WRONG. He should not have said that to me. But in my most polite voice I said, "Well, (you mother fucker) what a terrible thing to say!

You just paid money and I am going to entertain your ass and you are probably younger than me, BUT YOU LOOK OLDER!"

Everyone had a wonderful time. They all got drunk because drinks at the Elks are only $2.00 (who ever heard of a two-dollar drink?) We had so much fun. There was one young man there sitting all by himself in the middle of the audience…he was maybe in his late 30s. I went down to him, pulled up off his seat by his shirt, and screamed, "Oh my God, this is the youngest person here!"

That room full of people laughed for an hour and a half and during that time they could forget about having arthritis or any of their other problems. THAT IS WHY AT MY AGE, I AM STILL DOING THIS.

My life is full and on my tombstone I want it to read: GLITZ. GLAMOUR. COMEDY.

Let's face it. Drag has been around since Jesus was in that robe and I see the future for female impersonators as positive and prosperous. My advice to the young performers coming up is to find who you are and your own personal style. Don't be swayed by the latest fad or music or what other people may think of you. Keep the spectrum of the audience inclusive of all kinds of people out there in the world and keep the humor so that all can relate. Be people entertaining other people and you will go far. It is totally worth it.

Sometimes when we meet new people, I will hear them whisper to Roxy, "What shall we call him? Walter or Darcelle?"

Well, my friends, I can tell you now, right from the bottom of my heart, JUST CALL ME DARCELLE!

EPILOGUE
From the stage to a stagecoach

In the summer of 2010, I was asked to be Grand Marshall of Portland's Gay Pride Parade. They called me and said I was going to ride on the Wells Fargo Stage Coach. I was so excited I couldn't stand myself. First of all to be Grand Marshall was such an honor, it would have been okay if they pulled me in a red wagon. But a stagecoach! I was going to sit up top with the driver "shot-gun" style and Roxy would ride inside.

When we arrived at the start of the parade route on Sunday June 20, I was in my best Old Wild West madame outfit of brilliant lavender and Roxy was in a fringed leather shirt, cowboy hat, and so much turquoise jewelry it was amazing he could stand up.

I was thinking that there would be a ladder to climb up to my seat or a cherry picker or even just a stack of crates nailed together...anything to get me from the ground to the top of that coach. But NO...I saw no help at all. The horses were already harnessed up to the coach and they were much bigger than I anticipated.

Now I don't like any animal that is bigger than me...whether it is elephants or stagecoach horses...but especially when their rear ends are pointed right where I have to climb. Maybe, I thought, they had some scientific way to boost me up that I didn't know about. There were four men tending the coach…a wagon master that I would sit next to on top and then three other men who walked along with the horses during the parade to keep them calm. The men took me over to the side of the wagon that was opposite where the driver would sit and told me what to do.

First I was to put my left foot on the hub of the wheel…that's the thing that holds the wheel on and sticks out about 6 inches…Then with my right foot, I was supposed to step up on top of the wheel itself, which was made of steel and very slick. It's a very good thing I was not wearing heels that day. Then I put my left foot on a piece of four-inch steel that was sticking out for a step higher up. Then I put my right foot on the footrest where my feet would be once I was sitting in the seat by the driver. And of course I was supposed to be pulling myself up each step of the journey. Were they kidding?

First of all, I was all dressed up and the dress was tight with a slit all the way up to my whatever. Then each step was so slick that I finally threw off my shoes so I would not slip. I kept yelling, "I can't do this, I can't do this." It seemed like 800 people were just standing around all silent and watching intently. It was like the hush of the gallery in a golf game right before Tiger Woods makes the putt…no one said a word and no one moved a muscle to help me.

The wagon master was already up in his seat and I did not want to give up so I finally told the other three guys that they had to help me…and not to go away… they said they would guide my feet and I said, "That's great but FOR CHRIST'S SAKE, PUSH!"

So one of the big strapping guys in a cowboy hat and big silver belt buckle took my butt…one cheek in each hand and got me up the first couple of steps. Then the driver reached down his arm and pulled me up and around and of course I was facing the wrong way toward the back of the damn thing. When I finally got turned around and sat down, those 800 silent people cheered for five minutes. It was the highlight of my career… my butt up in the air at the beginning of the gay pride parade.

The cowboy who pushed me up said, "I will never as long as I live forget pushing Darcelle's buns up in the air one after the other…my hands are famous"

Once I was up there, it was great. The parade was very emotional. I have been applauded all of my career…but this was amazing. For blocks and blocks people were screaming, waving their arms, and calling my name. We LOVE you, Darcelle! We love you, Darcelle!"

It took about an hour and a half to drive the entire parade route and end up on Front Avenue, where they had set up a place to celebrate. But as we got close, the stagecoach just kept on going…right past everybody at the end of the parade route, the coach got in the car lane going south and didn't stop.

We went under the Burnside Bridge, under the Morrison Bridge, and ended up under the Hawthorne Bridge in the field where their truck was parked. They had to undo the horses before I could get down. This time they had a three-step ladder but it was not high enough of course, so I am hanging on and they are saying "Okay, you've got another foot to go" but they helped me down and it was much easier. Then they put the horses in the trailer and away they went. There we were looking glamorous, standing all alone in the middle of the park with no visible signs of support.

So the Wild West Madame and her cowboy cohort marched on over to the Marriot Hotel, had a couple of drinks, and then took at cab to the end of the Parade Route where everyone was waiting. More cheers when we arrived. We had gotten to the parade gathering place at 11:00 that morning and at 7:30 we got back to the club, washed our faces, changed our clothes, and went out to my daughter's for Father's Day.

Just another day for Darcelle.